English for
the Automotive Industry

Mike Berwald

D1731606

Dieses Buch als E-Book nutzen:
Use this book as an e-book:
mein.cornelsen.de

446z-5g-pgzg

Cornelsen

English for
the Automotive Industry

Autor: Mike Berwald
Beratende Mitwirkung: Amanda Welfare
Redaktion: Robert Baltzer
Redaktionelle Mitarbeit: Stephanie Hempel (extern)

Umschlaggestaltung: Studio SYBERG, Berlin
Umschlagfoto: Shutterstock.com/metamorworks
Layoutkonzept: Studio SYBERG, Berlin
Layout und technische Umsetzung:
PER MEDIEN & MARKETING GmbH, Braunschweig

Bildquellen:
S. 3/1: Shutterstock.com/Gorodenkoff; **S. 3/2:** Shutterstock.com/Frame Stock Footage; **S. 3/3:** Shutterstock.com/mentatdgt; **S. 3/4:** Shutterstock.com/Eugene_Photo; **S. 3/5:** Shutterstock.com/Avigator Fortuner; **S. 3/6:** stock.adobe.com/ViDi Studio; **S. 5/1:** Shutterstock.com/Gorodenkoff; **S. 5/2:** Shutterstock.com/Frame Stock Footage; **S. 5/3:** Shutterstock.com/mentatdgt; **S. 5/4:** Shutterstock.com/Eugene_Photo; **S. 5/5:** Shutterstock.com/Avigator Fortuner; **S. 5/6:** stock.adobe.com/ViDi Studio; **S. 6/oben mitte:** Shutterstock.com/Gorodenkoff; **S. 8/unten rechts:** Shutterstock.com/Kaspars Grinvalds; **S. 9/1:** Shutterstock.com/ImageFlow; **S. 9/2:** Shutterstock.com/Gorodenkoff; **S. 9/3:** Shutterstock.com/algre; **S. 9/4:** Shutterstock.com/Toyakisphoto; **S. 9/5:** stock.adobe.com/vodolej; **S. 9/6:** Shutterstock.com/fizkes; **S. 9/7:** Shutterstock.com/Gorodenkoff; **S. 9/8:** Shutterstock.com/pics721; **S. 9/9:** Shutterstock.com/Fahroni; **S. 13/oben rechts:** Shutterstock.com/Blue Planet Studio; **S. 14/o.:** Shutterstock.com/Frame Stock Footage; **S. 14/u.l.:** stock.adobe.com/Sergio Martínez; **S. 14/u.m.:** stock.adobe.com/Andrus Ciprian; **S. 14/u.r.:** stock.adobe.com/Andrus Ciprian; **S. 15/mitte rechts:** Shutterstock.com/Gorodenkoff; **S. 16/1, 3, 5, 7, 8:** stock.adobe.com/prism graph; **S. 16/2;9:** Shutterstock.com/stellarstock; **S. 16/4:** Shutterstock.com/Net Vector; **S. 16/6:** Shutterstock.com/Smartha; **S. 18/unten rechts:** Shutterstock.com/Gorodenkoff; **S. 20/mitte rechts:** Shutterstock.com/Gorodenkoff; **S. 21/mitte links:** Shutterstock.com/metamorworks; **S. 22/1:** Shutterstock.com/Prostock-studio; **S. 22/2:** Shutterstock.com/Hodoimg; **S. 22/3:** Shutterstock.com/Monkey Business Images; **S. 22/o.:** Shutterstock.com/mentatdgt; **S. 25/oben rechts:** Shutterstock.com/ANAID studio; **S. 28/unten rechts:** Shutterstock.com/Gorodenkoff; **S. 29/oben rechts:** Shutterstock.com/stoatphoto; **S. 30/o.:** Shutterstock.com/Eugene_Photo; **S. 30/u.:** Shutterstock.com/bbgreg; **S. 33/mitte rechts:** Shutterstock.com/fizkes; **S. 35/mitte:** stock.adobe.com/dmindphoto; **S. 37/mitte links:** Shutterstock.com/24Novembers; **S. 38/o.:** Shutterstock.com/Avigator Fortuner; **S. 38/u.:** Shutterstock.com/Sansoen Saengsakaorat; **S. 39/mitte rechts:** Shutterstock.com/Cagkan Sayin; **S. 45/mitte links:** Shutterstock.com/Inkoly; **S. 46/o.:** stock.adobe.com/ViDi Studio; **S. 46/u.:** Shutterstock.com/Andrey_Popov; **S. 51/oben mitte:** Shutterstock.com/PeopleImages.com - Yuri A; **S. 52/m.:** Shutterstock.com/Ferdinan84; **S. 52/m.l.:** Shutterstock.com/Julio Jodan; **S. 52/m.r.:** Shutterstock.com/Nazia Sara; **S. 53/mitte links:** Shutterstock.com/Vladimir Sukhachev; **S. 55/unten mitte:** stock.adobe.com/LeArchitecto; **S. 56/oben mitte:** stock.adobe.com/LeArchitecto; **S. 57/unten rechts:** Shutterstock.com/Julio Jodan; **S. 59/unten mitte:** stock.adobe.com/LeArchitecto; **S. 60/oben mitte:** stock.adobe.com/LeArchitecto; **S. 61/unten rechts:** Shutterstock.com/Ferdinan84; **S. 63/mitte rechts:** Shutterstock.com/Nazia Sara.

www.cornelsen.de

1. Auflage, 1. Druck 2024

Basierend auf *English for the Automobile Industry* (ISBN 978-3-464-20348-4)

Alle Drucke dieser Auflage sind inhaltlich unverändert und können im Unterricht nebeneinander verwendet werden.

Druck: Mohn Media Mohndruck, Gütersloh

ISBN: 978-3-06-123275-7 (Kursbuch)
Produktnummer: 1100034914 (E-Book)

PEFC-zertifiziert
Dieses Produkt
stammt aus
nachhaltig
bewirtschafteten
Wäldern und
kontrollierten Quellen

PEFC/04-31-1033   www.pefc.de

TABLE OF CONTENTS

	TOPICS	LANGUAGE FUNCTIONS
 **1** **Working in the automotive industry** Page 6	• Roles and responsibilities • Planning meetings and schedules • Current and future car trends	• Describing your job and workspace • Managing discussions • Making predictions
 **2** **Design and development** Page 14	• Designing a car • The development process • Project management • Virtual meetings	• Describing cars and features • Explaining processes • Giving updates • Leading online meetings
 **3** **Working with business partners** Page 22	• Selecting suppliers • Writing specifications • Business trips • Meetings	• Giving presentations • Explaining requirements • Writing emails • Leading discussions
 **4** **Processes and production** Page 30	• Improving processes • The production line • Exterior and interior car parts	• Making suggestions • Talking about problems and solutions • Describing car parts
 **5** **Sustainability and performance** Page 38	• Sustainability in the car industry • Cultural intelligence • Financial performance	• Talking about goals • Telephoning • Presenting numbers
 **6** **Sales and marketing** Page 46	• Car-buying attitudes • Digital marketing • Customer experience • Planning a future car model	• Convincing and persuading • Making comparisons • Dealing with customers and handling complaints

INTRODUCING
ENGLISH FOR THE AUTOMOTIVE INDUSTRY

As you will know from your job, English plays an increasingly important role in international business communication. *English for the Automotive Industry* will provide you with the language you need for effective communication with colleagues, customers and business partners. It includes a large range of technical vocabulary dealing with important automotive trends and topics, key processes and common business situations.

English for the Automotive Industry contains the following components which are designed to help you learn effectively.

- The book's six units cover a comprehensive range of important topics in the automotive industry. As you can see from the table of contents on page 3, the aim is to give a broad overview of the language needed for working in the industry in a compact format.

- The wide range of exercises will introduce you to new language in realistic situations and provide you with ample opportunities to practice and learn key phrases and technical terms.

- The book encourages frequent discussion with other people in your English course. The discussion tasks are focused on giving you the opportunity to draw on your personal experience while practicing key language. The simulations and mediation activities in each unit allow you to actively practice phrases and vocabulary in relevant scenarios. They encourage you to use and adapt the language learned to perform tasks as you would in the real world.

- ◁)) The listening tasks in every unit present a broad range of accents to prepare you for the way English is spoken internationally. The recordings can be accessed using the **Cornelsen Lernen App** or the **webcode "reteye"** on **codes.cornelsen.de**.

- 🖳 The **Cornelsen Lernen App** offers interactive exercises, which practice and expand on the useful phrases provided in this book. They are designed as a resource for independent learning.

- The appendix includes partner files, transcripts of the audio recordings, an answer key, a phrase bank with all useful phrases from this book, an A-Z wordlist as a summary of the vocabulary boxes and a glossary explaining technical terms and differences between frequently used American and British automotive terms. It is designed to help you to use the book in your own time as a resource for independent learning and for reference purposes.

The needs analysis on the next page will help you in setting personal learning goals before you get started and in assessing your progress once you have worked through the book.

Best of luck with your English course.

Mike Berwald
and the Cornelsen editorial team

NEEDS ANALYSIS

English for the Automotive Industry is designed to improve your English-language skills for a wide range of tasks relevant to the automotive industry. However, you are in the best position to know which skills you need to develop most to help you in your work.

Have a look at the list below and spend a few minutes ticking the skills that you consider most important. Which do you want to prioritize and improve? Add other skills to the list that you would like to concentrate on.

need more practice
have made good progress

Business situations

Participate in meetings
Manage discussions
Give presentations
Write emails
Telephoning

Auto industry tasks

Technical discussions

Explain technical processes
Talk about technical requirements
Manage projects and timelines
Discuss technical problems and solutions

Technical vocabulary

New trends and car technologies
Car design and development
Automotive production
Sales and marketing

Try to keep the skills you want to improve in mind while working with the book. Once you have completed it, turn back to this page and assess your progress.

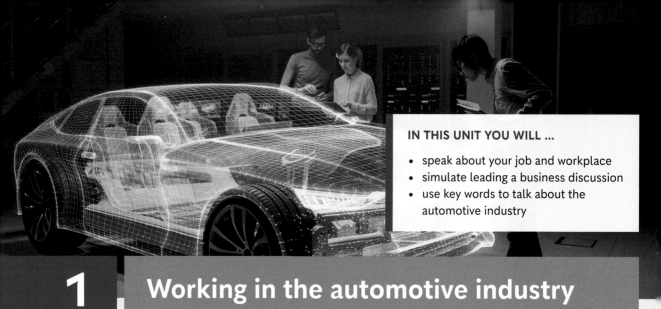

IN THIS UNIT YOU WILL ...

- speak about your job and workplace
- simulate leading a business discussion
- use key words to talk about the automotive industry

1 Working in the automotive industry

 Discuss the questions. Use the visuals and the Useful Phrases box to help you.

1 What area of the automotive industry do you work in?
2 What are some of your roles and responsibilities?
3 What stakeholders do you deal with at your job?
4 What has changed about your job since you started working in the industry? What do you think will change in the coming years?

Job Areas in the Automotive Industry

ROLES AND RESPONSIBILITIES	
Role	**Responsibility**
Fleet Sales Representative	Coordinates customer needs with the Production Department
Market Launch Coordinator	Makes sure products are ready for market introduction
Project Manager	Oversees project work packages and facilitates project workshops
Development Engineer	Responsible for making the concept, designing and testing a new product or component
Process Consultant	Consults and advises production facilities to improve their processes

USEFUL PHRASES

Describing your work and responsibilities
- I work in ... / the ... department.
- I'm responsible for ...
- One of my main tasks is ...
- I work closely with ...
- I deal with ...
- A lot has changed since ...
- I used to ... but now I ...

🔊
02

1 Listen to the dialogues and identify where they take place. Choose from the locations in the box.

automotive conference | business trip | office building | online project meeting | production facility

Location
Dialogue 1 _____
Dialogue 2 _____
Dialogue 3 _____
Dialogue 4 _____
Dialogue 5 _____

VOCABULARY

to **be on the right track** auf dem richtigen Weg sein
bottleneck Engpass
to **consult** beraten
day-to-day work tägliche Arbeit
directions (pl.) Wegbeschreibung
facility Einrichtung
to **facilitate sth** etw. moderieren
fleet customer Großkunde
to **participate in sth** an etw. teilnehmen
recommendation Empfehlung
requirement Anforderung
to **reschedule sth** etw. umplanen, verlegen
scheduling conflict Terminkollision

2 Fill in the missing information. If necessary, listen to the dialogues again to check your answers.

behind schedule | fleet customers | milestones | recommendations | requirements | right track | scheduling conflict | workflows

1 I'll prepare a report with my _____ and send it to you next week.

2 I think we are on the _____ .

3 One of Javier's main tasks will be to coordinate the _____ .

4 The workshops should also help us meet our project _____ .

5 I make sure our cars meet the technical _____ of each market.

6 I coordinate the needs of our _____ to the production department.

7 We need to discuss the timeline for the market launch. We are really _____ .

8 Tuesday at 3 pm seems to work – except for you. You have a _____ .

3 Match the sentence halves then discuss the questions below.

1 One of my tasks is to coordinate the
2 I participate
3 I work closely with external partners
4 I regularly deal with different
5 I sometimes facilitate
6 I often have to take
7 At my job I have to meet
8 One of my main tasks

a many deadlines and quality standards.
b including government authorities.
c on new tasks at my job.
d is finding new ways to improve our processes.
e workflow between the different sub-projects.
f project meetings or workshops.
g in online meetings nearly every day.
h departments at my job including sales and development.

1 Which of the sentences is true for your job?
2 For the sentences that aren't true for you, what departments/job areas could they apply to?
3 Can you think of other tasks you regularly do at your job that aren't included here? Give examples.

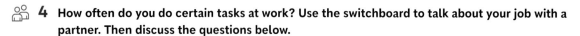

4 How often do you do certain tasks at work? Use the switchboard to talk about your job with a partner. Then discuss the questions below.

Example: *I regularly have to participate in meetings but I only have to facilitate workshops once a month.*

I	often sometimes regularly rarely never	have to need to	check | coordinate | consult | deal with | discuss | facilitate | hold | improve | meet | participate in | prepare | set up | work closely with | write	customers | deadlines | documents | emails | government authorities | meetings | milestones | presentations | processes | projects | requirements | schedules | suppliers | tasks | workflows | workshops	every day/week once a month/year every Monday/Friday

1 Which tasks do you like most about your job?
2 Which do you like the least?

3 Can you find three similarities about your jobs?
4 How about three differences?

5 Vocabulary building: Fill in the missing forms.

The **stress pattern** (Betonung) for English nouns ending in "-tion" is always the same. Regardless of how long the word is, the stress is always on the second to last syllable:
<u>na</u>tion, invi<u>ta</u>tion, partici<u>pa</u>tion ...

Remember that adding "-ment" to a verb (e.g. to require → requirement) will not change the stress pattern:
to im<u>prove</u> → im<u>prove</u>ment ...

Noun	Verb
	to invite
	to recommend
preparation	
participation	
	to coordinate
improvement	
facilitation	

6 What time suits you? You need to set up a meeting with your partner next week to discuss a project. Follow the instructions in the partner files at the back of the book.

▷ Partner Files, File 1:
Partner A, page 54 | Partner B, page 58

> **VOCABULARY**
>
> **meeting minutes (pl.)** Protokoll
> to **postpone sth until** etw. verschieben auf
> **request** Anfrage
> to **suit so** jmdm. zeitlich passen
> to **take a day off** einen Tag freinehmen

7 Label the work areas. Then discuss the questions below.

closed office | cubicle | open plan office | proving grounds | sales floor |
shop floor | test bench | warehous | working from home

1 _____

2 _____

3 _____

4 _____

5 _____

6 _____

7 _____

8 _____

9 _____

1 Which photo(s) best describes your workspace? What aspects do they share?
2 Which workspace would you prefer to work in? Which would you least prefer? Give reasons.
3 Do you sometimes work from home or have more than one workplace? What are advantages and disadvantages of having a flexible workplace?

 8 How do you like to work? Fill out this survey and then add any other aspects that are important for you at work. Compare your results with a partner.

Work Environment Attitudes
How important are the following factors at work for you? (1: most important | 6: least important)

Work Environment Factors

- A good, flexible workspace
- Modern work equipment
- A flexible work schedule
- Employees having responsibility

- Challenging tasks
- Clear team goals and strategy
- _____
- _____

9 SIMULATION

Your team has hired a new colleague, who is going to help you with your day-to-day tasks.

Provide information about the topics in the column on the right so your new colleague has all the information needed to help you do your job.

- Workspace and work environment
- Responsibilities
- Current tasks
- Schedule, regular meetings
- People I deal with
- Deadlines/Project milestones

 10 Read these meeting minutes and label each topic with the correct headline.

Car Features of the Future | Electrification | Global Strategy |
New Technologies | Trends in Human Resources

Topic 1: _____

- To summarize, participants agree technological improvements (e.g. range extension and shorter charging times) are needed to increase customer acceptance.
- Product planning wants to shift more capacity to EV production. Sales has a different opinion, but participants reach a consensus to implement the plan.
- Sales department reports growth in some foreign markets is difficult because of new competition.

Topic 2: _____

- Market research says advanced infotainment systems and personal device connectivity are having a larger effect on car-buying attitudes.
- Autonomous driving can be a potential gamechanger in the long-term.

Topic 3: _____

- Products need to be better adapted to local markets.
- The purchasing and logistics departments share the opinion that the global supply chain is at risk.
- Sales reports gains in emerging markets.

Topic 4: _____

- Participants look at the advantages and disadvantages of different workplace strategies. The meeting facilitator notes the discussion is deviating from the topic. HR requests the topic to be rescheduled for the next meeting.
- Recruiting believes a more appealing work environment is needed to secure high-tech global talent.

Topic 5: _____

- IT is of the opinion that processes and tasks can continue to be optimized or automated with AI.
- Employees need new skills to use AI effectively.

VOCABULARY

advanced fortschrittlich
appealing ansprechend
artificial künstlich
to **be adapted to sth** an etw. angepasst sein
charging time Ladezeit
competition Wettbewerb
electric vehicle (EV) Elektrofahrzeug
emerging markets Schwellenmärkte
gamechanger bahnbrechende Änderung
to **optimize sth** etw. optimieren
purchasing Einkauf
range extension Reichweitenverlängerung
to **secure sth** etw. sichern
supply chain Lieferkette

11 Which of the statements are true according to the text in exercise 10? True False

1 Customers completely trust electric cars resulting in a high rate of acceptance.

2 Market growth is difficult because there is the same competition as in the past.

3 Connecting your mobile phone to car systems is a reason why customers buy cars.

4 Autonomous driving will have a large impact on the automotive industry.

5 Reports suggest that the delivery of some parts and materials is not secure.

6 One-size-fits-all is no longer a good strategy when selling cars globally.

7 High-tech global talent is difficult to find and a plan to attract young workers is needed.

8 Employees don't need training to use artificial intelligence effectively.

12 Find words in the text that mean the opposite of the following words.

1 basic: _____

2 to have no effect: _____

3 to be safe: _____

4 losses: _____

5 unattractive: _____

6 real, genuine: _____

13 Match the words to make expressions from the text.

1	range	a	talent
2	car-buying	b	intelligence
3	personal	c	markets
4	autonomous	d	chain
5	supply	e	attitudes
6	emerging	f	extension
7	global	g	driving
8	artificial	h	device

14 Have a look at the Useful Phrases box. Can you find expressions with a similar meaning in exercise 10? Add them to the lines below the Useful Phrases box.

> **USEFUL PHRASES**   **Leading discussions**
>
> **Asking for opinions**
> - How do you feel about this?
> - What's your opinion on …?
>
> **Giving opinions**
> - In my mind …
> - As far as I'm concerned …
>
> **Agreeing**
> - I agree with you on …
> - I feel the same way.
>
> **Disagreeing**
> - Sorry, I can't go along with you there.
> - I'm afraid I see things differently.
>
> **Expressing agreement**
> - We are in agreement that …
> - We are all of the same opinion.
>
> **Redirecting a discussion**
> - I'm afraid we are getting off topic. Let's get back to …
> - The discussion is getting side-tracked.
>
> **Comparing ideas**
> - Let's look at the pros and cons of each idea.
> - Let's compare the benefits and drawbacks.
>
> **Summarizing**
> - To sum up, …
> - In summary we can say that …

_____

_____

_____

Do you know any other phrases that you could add to the table?

Step 1: Create small groups and select the three most relevant trends from exercise 10 for you/your company.

Step 2: Select different discussion leaders for each trend. The discussion leader makes sure the group refocuses the discussion when needed, compares different ideas, and defines three actions for each trend.

Step 3: Discuss using the Useful Phrases from exercise 14.

Step 4: Document your ideas below.

Trend 1:	Trend 2:	Trend 3:
Discussion leader:	Discussion leader:	Discussion leader:
Action 1:	Action 1:	Action 1:
Action 2:	Action 2:	Action 2:
Action 3:	Action 3:	Action 3:

16 **Add the phrases from the box that are used to talk about the future to the correct columns.**

I'm absolutely sure | I'm confident | I'm convinced | I doubt | It's likely | It may be that | There's a chance that | It's improbable

Certain:

Probable:

Possible:

Unlikely:

👥 **17** **In groups, discuss the future car trends below in terms of how certain you are each trend will happen using the phrases from exercise 16. Then rank the trends according to un-/likelihood (1-10).**

- a In fünf Jahren verdienen Autohersteller mehr Geld mit datenverbundenen Dienstleistungen und Mobilitätsdienstleistungen als mit tatsächlichen Autoverkäufen.
- b In zehn Jahren arbeiten alle traditionellen Autohersteller mit High-Tech-Unternehmen zusammen.
- c In zwanzig Jahren werden mehr als die Hälfte der Autos online gekauft.
- d In dreißig Jahren kaufen die meisten Menschen statt Autos Auto-Abonnements.
- e In vierzig Jahren werden benzinbetriebene Motoren nicht mehr in Europa verkauft.
- f In fünfzig Jahren übertreffen Brennstoffzellenfahrzeuge Elektrofahrzeuge.
- g In sechzig Jahren fahren die meisten Taxis autonom.
- h In siebzig Jahren gibt es aufgrund von Auto-zu-Auto-Kommunikation keine Autounfälle mehr.
- i In hundert Jahren sind die meisten Taxis Flugautos.
- j In zweihundert Jahren beamt man sich, statt Auto zu fahren.

Paradigm Shift: Electrification

The electric car has been around for longer than you think. Did you know Ferdinand Porsche's first ever car design in 1898 was electric? Or that in 1900 one third of the cars in the US were battery powered? Cheaper production costs and the invention of the electric starter soon made petrol cars the more popular choice and it wasn't long before electric cars had all but disappeared from the roads.

Nearly a century later, improvements in battery technology along with Tesla, a brand solely created for electric vehicle production, have brought electric cars back. Strict emission regulations to lower carbon and other harmful emissions have helped too. Whereas electric car sales were less than 1% of total global sales in 2010, in 2020 they accounted for over 10%. Future predictions estimate that by 2040 50% of vehicles on the road will be electric.

Even as electric vehicles (EVs) are expected to overtake internal combustion engines (ICEs) in the coming decades, there are still major hurdles ahead. To start with is the actual environmental benefit that electrification has come to represent. While it is true that EVs are generally greener when it comes to harmful emissions, a lot of that benefit depends on the energy mix the vehicle is charged with. Another issue is the environmental impact of battery production.

In terms of customer acceptance another obstacle to overcome is range anxiety, as actual driving distance can vary depending on a number of factors, including outside temperature, the terrain and other factors. Obviously a robust and widespread charging infrastructure to allow consumers to recharge easily and quickly will also help EVs become mainstream.

One challenge carmakers face is the dual task of reskilling workers and attracting new talent to develop EVs. Such specialists are in high demand, not only from traditional competitors, but from other business sectors as well.

Electrification still has a long way to go, and while the road ahead is not without its potholes, the future of EVs still appears to be quite bright.

VOCABULARY

to **be expected to do sth** es wird erwartet, dass …
to **estimate** einschätzen
greener umweltfreundlicher
harmful schädlich
hurdle Hürde
in terms of sth hinsichtlich etw.
to **overtake sth** etw. überholen
pothole Schlagloch
range anxiety Reichweitenangst
reskilling Umschulen
whereas wohingegen
widespread weit verbreitet

1 **What are the biggest challenges facing electrification in your opinion?**
2 **Has electrification impacted your job? Do you think it will in the future?**
3 **What can be done to make EVs sustainable?**
4 **Would you buy an electric vehicle? Why or why not?**

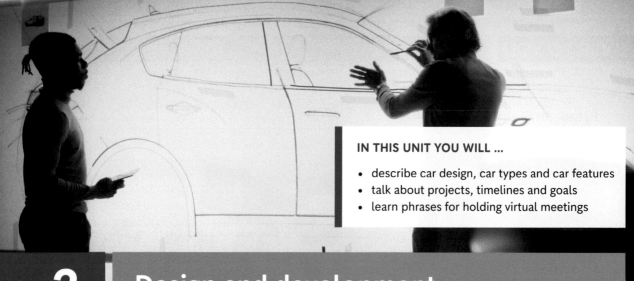

IN THIS UNIT YOU WILL ...

- describe car design, car types and car features
- talk about projects, timelines and goals
- learn phrases for holding virtual meetings

2 | Design and development

Complete the table and share it with a partner. Use the vocabulary box to help you.

	Your first car	Your current car	Your next car
Features			
Powertrain			
Drive			
Favorite memory			

VOCABULARY

all/four-wheel drive Allradantrieb
base model Basismodell
to **be equipped with sth** mit etw. ausgestattet sein
to **be fully-loaded** voll ausgebaut sein
electric elektrisch

front-wheel drive Vorderradantrieb
gasoline (AE) / **petrol** (BE) Benzin
powertrain Antrieb
rear-wheel drive Hinterradantrieb

🔊 03 **1** Listen to a meeting between a studio engineer, an exterior stylist and an exterior stylist team leader. Circle the words in *italics* that make the sentence true.

1 Gerhart says *none / both / only one* of the drag and lift coefficient(s) are/is too high.
2 Anna believes altering the hood design *compromises / compares / improves* the design language.

3 The roofline can't be lowered because the interior design team needed to improve the *headspace / headroom / leeway* in the car.

4 David suggests lowering the spoiler by five millimeters and extending the rear bumper by *five / fifteen / fifty* millimeters.

5 Gerhart is worried that making the rear bumper longer could affect the car's segment *class / classification / cabin*.

6 Anna believes nearly every successor is *lower / longer / lighter* than its predecessor.

7 Gerhart wants to make sure the solution works with the other design *platforms / options / parameters*.

8 David believes the timeline is very *flexible / narrow / tight*.

9 Gerhart has a plan to save time during the *design / development / distribution* phase.

VOCABULARY
boundary conditions Randbedingungen
cabin Fahrgastraum
crucial wichtig
drag coefficient Luftwiderstandsbeiwert
feasibility Machbarkeit
fender Kotflügel
grille Kühlergrill, Gitter
headroom Kopffreiheit
leeway Spielraum
lift coefficient Auftriebsbeiwert
predecessor Vorgängermodell
rear bumper hinterer Stoßfänger
successor Nachfolgermodell
wind tunnel Windkanal
windscreen angle Winkel der Windschutzscheibe

2 **Match the words to create expressions from the dialogue above.**

1 to lower	a an issue
2 to alter	b some simulations
3 to affect	c leeway
4 to solve	d the feasibility
5 to have	e the hood design
6 to run	f the safe side
7 to check	g the spoiler by five millimeters
8 to be on	h the segment classification

 3 **What makes a car design attractive? Place the words from the box under the correct heading. Then discuss the questions below with a partner.**

acoustics | shoulder line | dashboard | ergonomics | fenders | grille | headroom | headlights | HMI (human machine interface) | roofline | spaciousness | taillights | user experience (UX) | windscreen angle

Exterior design features		Interior design features	

1 Which exterior design features do you like the most? Give examples from car models you know.

2 What do you look for when it comes to cabin design and interior styling? Give examples.

3 What other features do you find important in car design? Add your ideas to the box.

4 With a partner, label the car types and discuss the questions below.

convertible | coupe | crossover | minivan (AE) / MPV (BE) | sedan (AE) / saloon (BE) | sports car | station wagon (AE) / estate car (BE) | sub-compact | SUV

1 _____

2 _____

3 _____

4 _____

5 _____

6 _____

7 _____

8 _____

9 _____

1 What are the advantages and disadvantages of each car type in your opinion?
2 What car type is your favourite? Why?
3 Which car types would you never buy? Why?

5 Match the opposites.

1 automatic	a base model
2 front-wheel	b sluggish
3 fully-loaded	c compact
4 quiet	d rough
5 responsive	e manual
6 sleek	f rear-wheel
7 smooth	g boxy
8 spacious	h noisy

DID YOU KNOW?
While people on both sides of the Atlantic enjoy driving the same kinds of vehicles, they often use **different names** to describe them. So while people in the United States talk about "sedans", people in Britain refer to "saloons". Similarly, drivers in the US refer to their "station wagon" while British motorists say "estate car". Or while in the US you might drive a "minivan", in Britain it's called an "MPV" (multi-purpose vehicle). Have a look at the complete American and British automotive glossary on page 79.

6 Complete the table below with words from above.
Then take turns describing the vehicles in exercise 4 to a partner using the language below.

exterior design	interior design	handling	ride	drive system	paint surface
rugged	luxurious	agile	smooth	all-wheel	metallic
distinctive	_____	_____	rough	_____	matte

7 Read through the car development steps in the box and add them to the gaps. Then order the steps correctly (1–10).

concept freeze | concept phase | construction release | customer phase | design freeze | part and vehicle testing | production trial | purchasing release | system release | virtual validation

a The _____ means the design is accepted and the vehicle meets all technical and functional requirements.

b The _____ confirms the vehicle fulfills the specification manual and all safety requirements.

c During the _____ stage all parts are tested and approved in a virtual environment.

d Next, the _____ permanently sets the technical data and specification manual. This milestone is more specific than the concept freeze.

e The _____ means series tools, equipment and part samples can be ordered.

f Virtual testing continues after the two "freezes".

The _____ means all interior and exterior car systems meet the needed requirements. Individual part testing continues.

g Finally, the _____ prepares the car for series production.

h In the _____ , the design and development departments work closely together. The car's styling and packaging are set.

i The next step is _____ in a real environment.

j The first step for a new vehicle is the

_____ . It includes gathering customer data, looking at the competition and choosing the powertrain. Topics like budget and pricing are also determined.

8 Are the following sentences true or false? Rewrite the false statements to make them true.

	True	False
1 The customer phase doesn't focus on how much the new car will cost.		
2 The customer phase decides whether the car has an electric motor or combustion engine.		
3 The concept phase decides how spacious the interior will be.		
4 The technical data can be changed after the design freeze.		
5 All parts are validated before the design freeze.		
6 All parts have been tested in a real environment before the purchasing release.		
7 Part samples are first ordered when all parts have been virtually validated.		
8 The production trial comes before series production.		

9 Vocabulary building: Fill in the missing forms.

Generally the **stress pattern** (Betonung) for verbs with two syllables is on the second syllable: con**firm**, e**quip** and ful**fill**.
One exception to the rule is **pur**chase, which stresses the first syllable. A good tip to keep in mind is that the second syllable "-chase" rhymes with "us" and not "face".

Noun	Verb
confirmation	
	to equip
fulfillment	
	to purchase
release	
	to require
	to specify
validation	

10 Fill in the gaps with the correct form of the words from exercise 9.

1 The construction release _____ the car meets all safety requirements and fulfills the specification manual.

2 Every part has to _____ several requirements including heat and cold testing.

3 We ordered the part samples, tools and _____ to begin testing in a real environment.

4 All the technical data for the component is in the _____ manual.

5 After the _____ release, we received the part samples from our supplier.

6 The construction _____ means the car can be built in the production trial.

7 A vehicle has to meet all technical and functional _____ to go into series production.

8 During road testing the ride was smooth. We can _____ the new part.

 11 Look at the development steps. With a partner describe the steps in your own words. Use the Useful Phrases below to help you.

Customer Phase	Concept Phase	Concept Freeze	Design Freeze	System Release	Purchasing Release	Construction Release	Production Trial

USEFUL PHRASES

Describing processes
- Firstly ...
- Secondly ...
- Thirdly ...
- After that ...
- The next step is ...
- And then ...
- During this stage ...
- The main focus of the ... is ...
- The ... deals with ...
- Finally,
- The last stage is ...
- Last but not least is ...

12 Fill in the blanks with the correct form of the words in the box.

capture | contingency plan | delegate | deliverables | mitigate | prioritize | secure

1 It is important to try and _____ all of the project tasks at the beginning of a project.

2 The skills of project members need to be considered when _____ tasks.

3 One way to _____ project problems is to analyse potential risks before a project starts.

4 Often a project has an overall goal that is broken down into smaller _____ .

5 The ultimate success of a project depends on its results or _____ .

6 At the project beginning _____ your tasks, so time is spent on the most important jobs first.

7 If you discover a project risk, develop a _____ to fall back on if needed.

8 Make sure you _____ the resources you need before starting it!

13 Match the sentence halves.

1 The main goal of our project is
2 The scope of our project includes the
3 One major project constraint we have is
4 Unfortunately in the planning stage,
5 Our project is currently on track,
6 To make sure our deliverables are on time,
7 When staffing the project we analysed
8 In terms of the budget,

a we set mini-milestones to track our progress.
b we didn't plan enough time for unforeseen events.
c but the upcoming milestones will be challenging.
d the skills we needed and found the right people.
e we didn't secure enough resources at the beginning.
f dashboard development but not the HMI.
g a very tight timeline.
h developing the successor of the Z9 model.

14 Read the following guideline. Then discuss the questions below with a partner.

How to plan and manage a project	
Goals and Scope • Determine goals and objectives • Define scope • Identify constraints / risks • Develop contingency plan if needed	**Timeline** • Set realistic timeline • Allow time for unforeseen events • Set milestones to check progress
Staffing and Resources • Identify skills needed • Estimate costs • Secure budget	**Work Packages and Deliverables** • Capture, prioritize and organize tasks • Create work packages • Ensure deliverables

VOCABULARY

to **capture sth** etw. erfassen
constraint Einschränkung
contingency plan Notfallplan
to **delegate sth** etw. delegieren
deliverables (pl.) Projektergebnisse
to **mitigate sth** etw. abmildern
objective kurzfristiges Ziel
scope Umfang
staffing Besetzung
unforeseen unvorhersehbar

1 What do you like about working in projects and what is the biggest challenge?
2 Which of the four topics above creates the most problems in your opinion? Share your experiences.
3 What could be improved in project planning in your opinion?

15 SIMULATION _____

Form small groups. Each person prepares a status report of a project they are working on. Use the following templates and the phrase beginnings from exercise 13 to help you.
Then present them to each other.

Goals & Scope

- Project goals
- Scope
- Constraints
- ...

Staffing & Resources

- Project team
- Budget
- Skills
- ...

Timeline

- Current status
- Upcoming milestones
- Overall timeline
- ...

Tasks & Work Packages

- Important tasks
- Work packages
- Deliverables
- ...

 16 MEDIATION _____

Step 1: Form small groups of 3–4 people and divide the participants into two sides: Nextron Motors and NextGen Software.

Step 2: Your companies are working together on a new car project. You are just about to begin your weekly status meeting when each of you receive an urgent email from your respective management teams.

Step 3: To prepare yourself for the online meeting, turn to the Partner Files (File 2): Partner A, page 54 | Partner B, page 58.

▷ **Step 4:** Hold the meeting. Refer to the Useful Phrases from the box below and those on page 11 to help guide you to a successful solution.

Step 5: Prepare a short email summary of your meeting results in German for your respective management teams.

USEFUL PHRASES   **Holding virtual meetings**

Welcoming participants
- Nice to meet you!
- Let's wait a few moments until everyone arrives.
- I think we can get started.

Connection issues
- Can everyone hear me okay?
- Sorry, I didn't catch that. The connection was bad.
- I am going to turn off my camera if that's OK.

Typical situations
- I'm afraid, your microphone is muted.
- Shall we use the hand signal when we want to speak?
- Could you post that in the chat, please?

Wrapping up
- Well, I think we've covered about everything, haven't we?
- Sorry, I have another meeting!
- Thanks everyone! Have a nice rest of the day!

Inside or outside?

≡

Big engines and sporty designs are a thing of the past – car buyers in the future won't be looking under the hood or at a sloping roofline when making the final decision on their next car, they will be looking at the inside of it. According to many industry experts electrification isn't the only major shift going on in the industry, car-buying attitudes are changing too.

But is it really true that features like handling, horsepower and a sleek design are a thing of the past? Are cars no longer bought for how fast you can go, but for what you can do in them? Not so fast. Price, product quality and vehicle performance still top most lists of factors influencing car-buying decisions, but the trend towards interior features is growing. Cabin comfort, the human machine interface, personal device connectivity and safety are just some features growing in popularity.

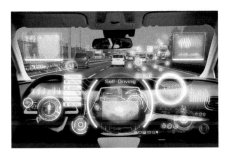

Higher comfort levels in the cabin may mean seats with more functions or next level automatic climate control systems, basically anything that can offer passengers more of a "living room" experience. A better human machine interface means easier cockpit navigation, like voice-controlled systems instead of switches or touch-screens. Seamless smartphone interfaces, high-resolution cameras and advanced infotainment systems are also of particular interest.

In addition to established safety features like blind spot detection, parking sensors and lane departure assistant, new car buyers are increasingly interested in the power of the connected vehicle like over-the-air maintenance updates and better traffic and road safety information. Car-to-car communication is also on the rise and already offered in high-end models. The idea is when more cars can "talk" with each other and with their surroundings (car-to-x) accidents will decrease. Another safety feature on the horizon is an augmented reality dashboard. Like a pilot's cockpit, they give drivers valuable information about their surroundings to help them drive safely.

One feature sure to disrupt the industry is the autonomous driving car. Besides changing the driving experience into a riding one and impacting how car interiors are designed, it could also affect car ownership too. Will cars still be bought when a fleet of self-driving cars is ready to take you wherever and whenever you want to go? Companies investing in "Car as a service" want to find out.

What exactly the future will look like is hard to say. One thing is for certain: Exterior and interior car features will keep evolving and shaping car-buying attitudes!

1 What features are you looking for when buying a car?
2 Do you think your attitude toward car buying will change? Why or why not?
3 Would you ride in a self-driving car?
4 Could you imagine not owning a car? Why or why not?

VOCABULARY

acceleration Beschleunigung
autonomous autonom
blind spot toter Winkel
high-end model Spitzenmodell
high-resolution hochauflösend
lane departure assistant Spurhaltesystem
seamless nahtlos
self-driving selbstfahrend
sloping abfallend

IN THIS UNIT YOU WILL ...

- learn language to select and correspond with external business partners
- talk about requirements and technical specifications
- learn skills for mediating a business meeting

3 | Working with business partners

**What external business partners do you work with?
Match the words from the box to the photos.
Then discuss the questions with a partner.**

service provider | supplier | vendor

Our company offers products to customers for sale, which means we are the last link in the economic chain. We typically have B2C (business to customer) relationships.	We provide other companies with goods or materials they need for their products and typically have just B2B (business to business) relationships.	Our company offers our products and services to individuals and other companies, which means we have both B2B and B2C relationships.

1 _____ 2 _____ 3 _____

1 Which vendors, suppliers and service partners do you work with?
2 What do you like about working with external business partners? What are some of the challenges?
3 Has the way you work with external partners changed since you started your job? Give examples.

 **1 Fill in the blanks with the words from the box.
Use a dictionary if necessary. Then act out the
dialogues with a partner.**

approach | negotiation | onboarding process |
request for proposal | specification manual |
terms and conditions

John: Sorry, I have a quick question about our _____ [1] for selecting new business partners.

Oliver: Sure! To start with you need to outline all of the technical details in a _____ [2].

John: I see. So you need to do that and write a _____ [3] that we send to the suppliers.

John: So, what happens after we recommend a new supplier?

Oliver: The procurement department conducts a _____ ⁴ with those suppliers who meet all technical requirements.

John: … and the _____ ⁵ are also set. Do we have an official _____ ⁶?

04

2 Compare John's and Oliver's notes. Then listen to the presentation and mark what is correct.

	John's notes		Oliver's notes	
Topic	Supplier Submission Process		Supplier Selection Process	
Preparing documents	First write a request for proposal then include it in a specification manual		First write a specification manual then include it in a request for proposal	
Evaluating suppliers	We are permitted to conduct questionnaires, visits, and checks		We must not conduct questionnaires, visits, and checks	
Product owner tasks	• Make sure supplier understands technical requirements • Evaluate offers objectively • Clearly document findings		• Make sure supplier aligns with technical requirements • Evaluate offers subjectively • Clearly document findings	
Negotiating / Onboarding	• Procurement negotiates contract • Formal process for onboarding		• Procurement negotiates contract • No formal process for onboarding	

> **VOCABULARY**
>
> to **align sth with sth** etw. auf etw. ausrichten
> **awarding** Vergabe
> to **be obliged to do sth** verpflichtet sein etw. zu tun
> **comprehensive** umfassend
>
> **merit** *hier:* Leistung
> **procurement department** Einkauf
> to **submit sth** etw. unterbreiten, vorlegen
> **suitable** passend, geeignet

3 Match the presentation functions from the box with the sentences. Then put the sentences in the correct order (1-6). Listen to the dialogue again if necessary or refer to the transcript on page 66.

Audience benefit | Goal of presentation | Presentation structure | Speaker introduction | Time/question policy | Welcoming participants

Order

a First, I'll talk about the steps needed to receive supplier proposals, next, your role as product owner in the evaluation phase and finally I'll outline the steps once the procurement department receives the evaluation of the supplier.

b As I'm only talking for five minutes, I'd be happy to answer any questions at the end.

c Good morning, it's great to be here.

d I am Sébastien Leroi from the Procurement Department.

e The purpose of today's talk is to explain our approach for identifying, evaluating and selecting suppliers.

f Afterwards you should have a clear overview of the phases of the selection process and a deeper understanding of your role as product owner.

Presentation functions

a _____

b _____

c _____

d _____

e _____

f _____

4 Match the words to find the collocations that were used in the dialogue.

1	to align	a	a proposal
2	to assess	b	the contract
3	to award	c	offers fairly
4	to distribute	d	a quick and smooth transition
5	to ensure	e	the request for proposal to potential suppliers
6	to submit	f	with the technical requirements

5 With a partner, give an introduction of the Supplier Selections Process in your company using the phrases from exercise 3 and the Useful Phrases on page 18.

6 Complete the following sentences using the correct form of the words from the box.

may not | must | need | needn't | oblige | permit | require | should

1 As a product owner, company policy _____ you to outline the standards, expectations, and requirements for the products or services in a specification manual.

2 You _____ write the RFP yourself, much of it is a standard document.

3 After the submission phase, the offers _____ be evaluated.

4 In the evaluation phase you are _____ to conduct questionnaires, site visits, and reference checks to make a complete evaluation.

5 A product owner _____ to make sure all offers have been understood and are aligned with the technical requirements.

6 You are _____ to assess each proposal fairly and only based on its technical merits.

7 You _____ use costs as a decision-making criteria.

8 Although there is no formal onboarding process, a list of recommendations _____ be followed to help ensure a quick and smooth work integration.

7 Categorize the words from the box by placing them into the correct column.

allow | don't have to | forbid | have to | must not | not allow | prohibit | supposed to

necessary	not necessary	against the rules	recommended or allowed

Look at the words from the box in exercise 6 and add them to the table.

8 Match the English word to the German translation.

1	Halterung	a	scope
2	Aufragnehmer*in	b	durability
3	Abweichung	c	bracket
4	Strapazierfähigkeit	d	objective
5	Heckklappe	e	contractor
6	Zielsetzung	f	deviation
7	Musterteil	g	tailgate
8	Umfang	h	sample

9 What goes into a specification manual? Use the words from exercise 8 to complete this technical specification.

Title: This specification manual describes the functions, requirements and test conditions the product and the _____ [1] need to fulfill.

_____ [2]: The development of a _____ [3] for the tailgate of car project BZ432.

_____ [4] **of offer:** The contractor must agree to satisfy all the quality requirements. Before selection, the contractor may be audited and must be approved by the customer's evaluation standards.

Timeline: The delivery dates have to be met according to the car project plan.

_____ [5] **parts:**
• 3 sets of parts for functional testing
• 3 sets of parts for vehicle integration tests

Data exchange: The product is for internal use only.

Quality: All company quality documents in the specification manual need to be fulfilled.

Requirements: Any _____ [6] requires the approval of the customer.

Test requirements: The part must pass all functional, _____ [7], and climate tests.

Functionality: This bracket connects the lifting mechanism on the _____ [8] to the car body.

10 Looking at exercise 9, decide whether the following statements are true or false.

	True	False
1 The specification manual describes only the requirements the part must fulfill and not the contractor.		
2 The contractor can be audited only after the awarding of the contract.		
3 Several sets of sample parts are needed for testing.		
4 Data used for developing the part may be exchanged with external business partners.		
5 A deviation from the accepted quality requirements must be approved by the customer.		
6 The contractor is allowed to determine its own test requirements.		
7 The part is not permitted to fail any of the tests.		
8 The bracket to be developed is located in the back of the car.		

11 **Who is responsible for what? Use the switchboard to talk to a partner about the job requirements involved when working with external partners. Then answer the questions.**

Example: *The product owner has to assess the offers fairly.*

The product owner The contractor The purchaser The product	has to must (not) should need(s) to	align with | approve | assess | conduct | deliver | distribute | document | fulfill | meet | pass | outline | satisfy | submit	all any the	deviations | evaluations | negotiation | objectives | offer(s) | parts | project plan | quality requirements | RFP | samples | tests	fairly on time clearly

1 Can you think of any other requirements that need to be fulfilled at your company?
2 Which requirement do you think is the most difficult to fulfill?

12 SIMULATION —————————————————————————————————

Step 1: Create small groups of 3-4 people. Split the roles evenly between customer and contractor.

Step 2: Hold a meeting using the agenda on the right to set up ground rules for your collaboration. Use the words from exercise 7 and the Useful Phrases on page 11 to help you. Make sure you decide between what is necessary, not necessary, against the rules, and recommended or allowed.

Step 3: After your meeting, discuss how it went.
- What points of the meeting went well?
- Which areas were difficult?
- What could have helped to make things easier?

Meeting agenda: Project collaboration

- Regular project communication
- Availability / Response time to emails
- Delivery schedule
- Quality assurance
- Dealing with problems
- Sharing data with other companies
- Performance monitoring
- Sending and storing data
- Documentation and record-keeping

13 **How do you usually correspond with business partners? Read the following email and fill in the missing information.**

best regards | do not hesitate | due to | hope | in regards to | unfortunately | we would appreciate

Dear Mr Martínez,

I _____ [1] this email finds you well.

I am writing _____ [2] the sealing on the tailgate. During testing we

_____ [3] had a problem with water entry. We believe it may be

_____ [4] the rubber sealing (see attachments). _____ [5] your

immediate attention concerning this matter. Please _____ [6] to contact me if you

need further information.

Thank you and _____ [7],
Markus Mueller

14 With a partner, discuss the function of each sentence in exercise 13. Then match the sentences with the functions by adding them to the table.

Function	Email 1 (exercise 13)	Email 2 (exercise 15)
Greeting		
Small talk		
Reason for email		
Request		
Future contact		
Sign Off		

15 Connect the phrases to create an email response to exercise 13. Then add them to the table in exercise 14. With a partner, discuss which email is more formal. Give reasons for your answer.

1 Hello	a if you have any further questions.
2 I hope you	b regards,
3 I'm writing about the water entry issue.	c drawings to confirm our theory?
4 Can you please send us more	d We believe it may be due to the wrong sealant.
5 Feel free to get back to me	e Markus,
6 Kind	f are doing well.

Your testing department has shown the cause of the water entry is not an improper sealant and you need to resolve the issue with Sealtex immediately. Discuss the questions.

1 Would you send an email, set up a phone call or video call, or arrange a face-to-face meeting?
2 What are the advantages and disadvantages of these communication forms?

16 Complete the business traveler's blog by adding the missing prepositions.

I was travelling to the airport _____ ¹ train when it broke down and I missed my flight. My colleague, who was supposed to pick me _____ ², had already left so I took a taxi to the plant. I was not _____ ³ time for the meeting, but luckily I was _____ ⁴ time to catch the product presentation. After the meeting our business partners showed us _____ ⁵ their production facility. The next days went much better! On Tuesday, we met _____ ⁶ our business partners for dinner. So tasty! After our last meeting our business partners took us to check _____ ⁷ some of the local sights before dropping us _____ ⁸ at the airport. All is well that ends well!

With a partner, think about your last business trip and answer the following questions.

1 Where and when did you go?
2 Why did you go?
3 How did you travel? Did anything interesting happen on the journey?
4 Who did you meet?
5 What happened during the trip? Was it all business or did you do some sightseeing?
6 Was the trip successful? Why or why not?

17 How do you lead effective discussions? Match the sentence halves and discuss the questions with a partner.

1 Let's remember our main objective	a I've understood so far …
2 I think it is a valid point,	b you're saying something similar to John.
3 I'm afraid we are going in	c your last idea a bit more?
4 Could you expand on	d from another perspective.
5 These are the main points	e is to reach an agreement.
6 If I understood you correctly,	f where you are coming from.
7 I can see	g but let's come back to the main issue.
8 Let's look at this from	h circles on this issue.

1 Which of these sentences are used to refocus a discussion? _____

2 Which sentences signal active listening? _____

18 MEDIATION _____

Step 1: Create small groups of 3 or 4 people and read the text to the right.

Step 2: Select meeting roles from the Partner Files (File 3) and review your role for the meeting:
- Partner A, page 55: Meeting Facilitator
- Partner B, page 59: CEO, Supplier Sealtex
- Partner C, page 62: Procurement Department, Nextron Motors
- Partner D, page 64: Development Engineer, Nextron Motors

Meeting for the Tailgate Sealing of the BZ432

The background: Climate testing on the tailgate sealing from the new model BZ432 revealed water entry problems. After email correspondence (exercises 13 and 15) the issue is still unresolved. A face-to-face meeting was called at Sealtex's headquarters and an external mediator has been arranged to facilitate.

Step 3: Use the phrases from exercise 17 and the Useful Phrases below to hold the meeting. Document your results.

Step 4: After the meeting, write down what went well and what you would like to improve. Share your thoughts with your group. Ask at least one meeting member to give you feedback.

Step 5: Write a short email summarizing the meeting results. Use the six email functions from exercise 14 to help you. Compare your emails with the other meeting members.

USEFUL PHRASES Opening and closing meetings

Opening meetings
- Nice to see you all.
- Let's start with a round of introductions.
- Let's take a look at the agenda.
- Shall we move on to the first item?

Closing meetings
- If there is nothing else, I think we can wrap it up.
- Let's recap what we have agreed on …
- Thanks for all contributing, the meeting was really constructive.

Moving up: Vertical integration is on the rise

≡

"Strength in numbers" has been the business strategy of carmakers for decades. A good example is Stellantis whose founders PSA and FiatChrysler had already experienced several mergers on their own before joining forces to bring sixteen brands under one roof in 2019. They followed this strategy, known as horizontal integration, for a simple reason: by expanding its size, a company can increase market share, diversify their product offer and save money by economies of scale.

Recently, however, carmakers have been focusing on vertical integration, which means the strategy of controlling more than one phase (supplier, manufacturer, vendor and distributor) of their value chain before their product reaches a customer. The goal of vertical integration is to reduce costs, be more independent and potentially gain new profit sources. There are two types of vertical integration. "Backward", for example, refers to a manufacturer trying to control the phases before production instead of relying on suppliers. "Forward" would be controlling the phases after production, namely distribution and sales. Amazon is a good example of a company that has vertically and horizontally integrated. It started as a vendor but now produces some of its own products and distributes with its own delivery company.

When Tesla started to vertically integrate by producing its own parts in 2014, the strategy was questioned at the time. However, after a global chip shortage, the effects of the pandemic and the continuing struggle for raw materials, this strategy is now seen as a model for other companies. Now many OEMs (original equipment manufacturers) have established their own battery plants and software centers.

There are, however, many challenges: Firstly, vertical integration forces a company to work with economies of scale and requires a large initial investment, which limits a company's financial flexibility. Another challenge is that companies need to learn the business on the fly. Success as a producer, for example, does not guarantee success as a supplier, distributor or vendor. Because of these challenges it is highly unlikely companies will completely vertically integrate. The challenge for companies in the future will be to find the right balance to stay competitive!

1. What are the differences between horizontal and vertical integration? Explain in your own words.
2. What are the four roles in the value chain before a product reaches a customer? Explain in your own words.
3. Do you know of any examples of vertical integration at your company?
4. In what areas would vertical integration (or doing tasks in-house) make sense at your company in your opinion? Where would outsourcing make more sense?

VOCABULARY

competitive wettbewerbsfähig
economies of scale (pl.) Skaleneffekte
to **expand sth** etw. ausweiten
merger Fusion
on the fly spontan, ohne Vorbereitung
shortage Knappheit
struggle Ringen, Kampf
value chain Wertschöpfungskette

IN THIS UNIT YOU WILL ...

- describe production processes and suggest improvements
- learn language for talking about problems and discussing solutions
- acquire vocabulary for car parts and their characteristics

4 Processes and production

 Have you heard of the "Toyota Production System"? Read the text and discuss the questions below with a partner.

The "Toyota Production System" is used by many companies today to optimize production processes. According to the system there are three main areas that cause processes to be inefficient:

MURI

Overburdening:
The process is expected to do too much, leading to problems (stressed workers, machine breakdowns)

MURA

Unevenness:
The process performance fluctuates or the process does not flow consistently

MUDA

Waste:
Steps in the process are inefficient

1 Which of the three causes the most process problems in your opinion? Explain why.
2 Think of a process or workflow at your work that has changed. Did the change deal with one of these areas? Explain.
3 Can you think of a process or workflow at your job that could be better? Which of the three areas is the source of the problem?

VOCABULARY

to **fluctuate** schwanken
to **overburden sth** etw. überlasten
unevenness Ungleichmäßigkeit

1 Listen to a lean process consultant talk about the Toyota Production System and the 8 types of *muda*. Fill in the missing information.

05

Defects	Overproduction	Waiting	Not-utilized talent
Defects can lead to having to _____ 1 or rework parts.	A _____ 2 in production is having to rework more products.	Any step that slows down a process or creates a _____ 3.	An example on the _____ 4 is employees not receiving proper training.

Transportation	Inventory	Motion	Extra processing
This can result in more work, a higher _____ 5 and more machine wear and tear.	This type of waste includes the costs to _____ 6 materials, work in progress or even finished products.	_____ _____ 7 can better utilize their time if the tools they need are close at hand.	This includes anything that _____ 8 what the process and product requires.

> **VOCABULARY**
>
> **cycle time** Taktzeit
> to **exceed sth** etw. überschreiten
> to **rework sth** etw. überarbeiten
> to **scrap sth** etw. verschrotten
>
> **shop floor** Produktionsstätte
> to **stockpile sth** etw. bevorraten
> to **utilize sth** etw. verwerten, verwenden
> **wear and tear** Verschleiß

2 Match the sentence halves of these office waste examples. Then add the type of *muda* to them.

1 In the office, defects and poor quality	a a one-page summary is enough.	1 _____
2 This waste could be something as simple as making	b how to cut waste in their own work areas, which is potentially the biggest waste of all.	2 _____
3 There are many examples in office work, like long	c or making too many mouse clicks to find them.	3 _____
4 This waste includes not asking employees for their ideas	d response times for emails, ineffective meetings or decisions that take too long.	4 _____
5 An easy example of this waste is when	e waiting to be worked on and unused or out-of-date files.	5 _____
6 In an office it could be something as simple as files	f often result from work processes that are not standardized and stable.	6 _____
7 Time could be wasted having to search for files	g too many copies or creating lists or reports no one reads.	7 _____
8 An example might be preparing a detailed presentation when	h colleagues who often work together don't sit near each other.	8 _____

With a partner, explain *muda* in your own words. Can you give some examples from your own job?

3 In pairs, give each other advice on the following situations using the Useful Phrases below.

Partner A	Partner B
1 Your partner has to wait too long for decisions from his boss. 2 Your partner is wasting too much time searching for files. 3 Your partner's project results are not consistent. 4 A process your partner works with is inefficient but they don't know where the bottleneck is.	1 Your partner's team is wasting time because they sit in separate offices. 2 The roles in your partner's team aren't clear and often two employees are working on the same task. 3 Your partner spends too much time creating presentations no one reads. 4 Your partner needs better IT skills for their job.

USEFUL PHRASES **Making suggestions and recommendations**

- How about trying a different solution?
- Why don't we move our work stations closer?
- By removing this step, we could save time.

- I'd recommend reducing your inventory.
- What about standardizing the process?
- If I were you, I'd clarify the responsibilities.
- Couldn't we simplify this process?

4 Read this dialogue between a process consultant and a shop floor manager and fill in the blanks with the words from the box.

come up with | consider different | decide on | discover | implement | investigate | locate the cause of | solve

Mauro: What's the best way to locate the source of a process problem?

Petra: It's not easy. Often you first _____ [1] a problem by means of a knock-on effect like a higher cycle time. The first step is to _____ [2] the issue by checking the process from end to end.

Mauro: And when you _____ [3] it, what is the best way to solve it?

Petra: A good way is a simple brainstorming session. There you can _____ [4] different solutions to correct the problem.

Mauro: I see. I suppose it's best to _____ [5] solutions.

Petra: Right! Evaluate ideas in terms of cost, effectiveness, time and energy. Whatever criteria is the most relevant for you. And then _____ [6] one!

Mauro: And the last step is to _____ [7] it and track its effectiveness.

Petra: Exactly. Hopefully your solution will permanently _____ [8] the problem and it won't happen again!

Are the verbs above used to speak about problems or solutions? Categorize them.

Problems: _____

Solutions: _____

5 In pairs, read through the Useful Phrases. Can you add other phrases for talking about problems and solutions? Compare with the Answer Key on page 72.

USEFUL PHRASES Talking about problems and solutions

Describing problems
- We need to find the cause of the problem.
- What about looking at the full impact / any knock-on effects?
- We should assess the problem in terms of money / time / energy / stress.

Giving reasons
- It seems this option is more cost-effective.
- This approach would be more time-saving.
- It could be much easier to do it this way.
- I see your point, but this idea would be more time-consuming.

Finding solutions
- Shall we hear other solutions before making a decision?
- How about considering the problem from a different angle?
- Let's evaluate our ideas based on costs / effectiveness / time / energy.

- I'm afraid this solution is much more cost-intensive.
- Doing it this way would be more labour-intensive.

 6 MEDIATION

Step 1: Each person should think of a process or workflow they work with that could be optimized. Break down the most important information on the process/workflow in English.

Step 2: Create small groups. Explain the process and the problem or waste that needs improvement to each other.

Step 3: As a group, select one of the processes presented in Step 2 to improve.

Step 4: Discuss possible improvements according to the guideline on the right. Use the Useful Phrases above to help you.

Step 5: Discussion debriefing: What worked well and what could have been better?

Kontinuierlicher Verbesserungsprozess

1 Begrenzen Sie den Umfang: Welchen Prozess oder welches System möchten Sie genau verbessern?
2 Beschreiben Sie die aktuelle Situation: Was ist das Problem? Wie haben Sie es entdeckt? Wie oft tritt es auf?
3 Bewerten Sie das Problem: Quantifizieren Sie das Problem in Bezug auf Geld, Zeit, Energie und/oder Stress.
4 Analysieren Sie das Problem: Was sind die Ursachen, Verbindungen oder Schnittstellen? Gibt es etwaige Folgeeffekte?
5 Brainstorming zu Lösungen.
6 Bewertung der Lösungen und Einigung.

7 What are the three production areas before the assembly called? Unscramble the words to find the names. Then add them to the table below.

boyd posh: _____   intpa hosp: _____   spers ophs: _____

Use the correct form of the words in the box to complete the table.

apply | assembly | blank | cure | gap | seal | treatment | weld

Production Area 1: _____			
Blanking Large metal sheets are cut into smaller pieces called _____ ¹ for specific parts.	**Stamping** Blanks are then stamped using dies and presses to form body panels and frame parts.	**Piercing** Holes or features are created in stamped parts needed for connections in the _____ ².	**Trimming & Quality Check** Extra material is cut off and parts are inspected for quality.

Production Area 2: _____			
Body Assembly Stamped parts are _____ ³ or otherwise joined to form the basic vehicle structure.	**Frame Alignment** The assembled body is checked to ensure proper alignment and structural integrity.	**Panel Fitting & Subassemblies** Body panels are fitted; _____ ⁴ and alignments are adjusted. Doors and hoods are integrated into the body structure.	**Seam Sealing** Seams are _____ ⁵ to prevent corrosion and improve structural integrity.

Production Area 3: _____			
Surface Preparation The vehicle body is cleaned and receives _____ ⁶ to make sure the surface is clean and smooth.	**Primer** Primer is _____ ⁷ to improve adhesion, corrosion resistance and give a uniform surface for the next paint layers.	**Basecoat & Clearcoat** The actual vehicle color is applied. Next, a clear layer improves the gloss and durability and protects the basecoat from damage.	**Curing & Quality Check** To achieve the right hardness, the painted body is _____ ⁸. Inspections ensure the quality.

In groups of three, use the verbs below to explain one of the production areas each.

1 cut — stamp
  — pierce — inspect

2 weld and join
  — check — fit — seal

3 clean and treat
  — apply — protect
  — cure

VOCABULARY

adhesion Haftverbund
to **apply sth** etw. auftragen
assembly Montage
blank Zuschnitt
to **cure sth** *hier:* etw. aushärten
die *hier:* Pressform

gap *hier:* Fuge, Spaltmaß
primer Grundierung
seam Naht
to **stamp sth** *hier:* etw. stanzen
treatment Behandlung
to **weld sth** etw. schweißen

8 How many exterior parts do you know? Complete the overview in the Partner Files.

Partner Files, File 4: Partner A, pages 55-56 | Partner B, pages 59-60

9 Match the materials to the parts made from it. Do you know any other materials or parts?

1	steel	a	window, windshields, headlights, mirrors
2	plastic	b	seals, windshield wiper blades, tires
3	aluminium	c	bumpers, doors, roofs
4	rubber	d	grille, brackets, license plate holder
5	glass	e	door panels, the rocker panel, hood, tailgate
6	fiberglass	f	wheels, lightweight body parts

10 Find an image of a car you like and describe its exterior to a partner.

11 With a partner, describe the car interior on the photo. Use the Vocabulary box to help you.

Look for a photo of your own car's interior or look up a car interior you like. With a partner, take turns finding differences between the interiors.

VOCABULARY

accelerator Gaspedal
air vent Lüftungsdüsen
A-pillar A-Säule
brake pedal Bremspedal
center console Mittelkonsole
dashboard Armaturenbrett
door trim Türverkleidung
driver seat Fahrersitz
footwell Fußraum
glove compartment Hand-
    schuhfach
headliner Himmel
horn Hupe
instrument cluster
    Instrumententafel
passenger seat Beifahrersitz
rear-view mirror Rückspiegel
sun visor Sonnenblende

12 How are parts installed in the assembly? Connect the English word to the German translation. Then fill in the blanks with the correct form of a word and a preposition if necessary.

1	to bolt on	a	anschrauben
2	to bond to	b	anklemmen
3	to clip on	c	verschrauben
4	to rivet together	d	kleben
5	to screw to	e	montieren
6	to mount on	f	nieten

1 The robot _____ the windshield _____ the frame of the car.

2 Hang-on parts like doors, windows and other interior features are _____ the car.

3 An assembly line worker _____ the door trim _____ to the door.

4 One way to join two pieces of material is to _____ them _____ .

5 The assembly line worker _____ the dashboard _____ the car frame.

6 Assembly line workers _____ the wheels _____ to the car.

13 **What's the problem? Fill in the blanks of these common problems on the assembly line. Use a dictionary or the glossary at the back of the book if necessary.**

broken | dent | doesn't work | error | fitting problem | loose | scratch | torn

1 The front seat is _____ again. I can't understand why!

2 One of the connecting pins of the infotainment system is _____ again, so it is not working.

3 The paint surface of the last five cars has a _____. We need to find the cause!

4 The dashboard is not properly fixed to the car frame. Some of the screws are too _____.

5 We can't check the onboard computer. The diagnostic program has an _____.

6 This car has a _____ in the hood, we need to send it to the rework station.

7 The windshield wiper is defective, it _____.

8 There is a _____ with the new bumpers we received from the supplier.

14 SIMULATION _____

You and your partner work on the assembly line.

Each of you should select a problem from exercise 13 to discuss. Take turns interviewing each other using the checklist on the right to learn more about the problem and how your partner would solve it. Use phrases from exercises 4 and 5 to help you.

Checklist

1 How did you discover the problem?
2 What is the source of the problem?
3 How do you plan to solve it? (You can ask your partner for ideas.)
4 How will you implement the solution?
5 How will you track the solution to make sure the problem does not happen again?

15 **Read the rules for "Name that Part". Then play with your group.**

▷ **Step 1:** Create groups of 3-4 players. Each player uses a different template provided in the Partner Files.
Partner Files, File 5: Partner A, page 56 | Partner B, page 60 | Partner C, page 62 | Partner D, page 64

Step 2: Fill in the missing information for the five parts on your template.

Step 3: When everyone is ready to start, take turns describing the five car parts on your template by reading clues from left to right. Guess what part is described after each clue. Each player has two guesses per car part. You can use the words below for help.

Position	Characteristics	Shape
• exterior / interior • near the front end / back end of the car • above / below / next to the … • between the … and the …	• heavy / light • durable / fragile • stiff / flexible • weak / strong	• square • round • rectangular • triangular

Scoring is done as follows:
A player who guesses the part correctly after 1 clue = 3 points, 2 clues = 2 points, 3 clues = 1 point.
After 4 clues the person describing gets 1 point, after 5 clues = 2 points.

Good luck!

The Factory of the Future

≡

For years carmakers have focused on reducing waste and maximizing efficiency to stay competitive as production processes have become more and more complex. More model derivatives and higher levels of vehicle customization have constantly forced carmakers to be more flexible. Now original equipment manufacturers (OEMs) who produce both electric vehicles (EVs) and vehicles with internal combustion engines (ICEs) are facing an even greater challenge. As the demand for electric vehicles continues to grow, so too does the need for production lines to react quickly to market changes. Carmakers need to be able to quickly shift the number of EVs or ICEs that roll off their production lines. With the high costs of electric vehicles, a key to future success will be how efficiently this can be done.

Some experts think that the traditional way of assembling cars, where parts arrive in a specific order, won't work well for complex EVs. The unique features of EVs, such as their size, weight distribution, and battery placement, create fundamental differences in how they are made. An example of this is in the body shop where structural differences and EV crash test standards require different welding techniques. These technical differences often mean different processing times in the press shop, body shop and assembly. It also makes a standard cycle time needed for pearl chain production extremely difficult to achieve.

What is the solution? One idea being tested to deal with this complexity is the idea of "intelligent" products. This approach would have cars on automated trolleys that would convey them through a production hall and stop at various work cells. The car would "tell" robot vehicles what parts they need and the robots would bring the parts to the work cell. This, however, needs a complex network of workstations and a sophisticated level of automation and digitization.

As with other aspects in the automotive industry, the switch to electric vehicles is presenting production lines with new challenges. Car production will certainly change in the coming decade, the only question is how big those changes are going to be!

VOCABULARY

to **achieve sth** etw. erreichen
to **convey sth** *hier:* etw. transportieren
customization Anpassung, Personalisierung
derivative Derivat, Modellvariante
original equipment manufacturer (OEM) Automobilhersteller
pearl chain Perlenkette
sophisticated ausgefeilt
trolley Wagen

1 **What are the challenges of building EVs and ICEs at the same time? Explain in your own words.**
2 **Do you agree with the strategy to offer more and more derivatives and features or do you think a "less is more" strategy would be better? Give reasons.**
3 **What do you think is the best strategy to cope with the challenge of co-producing EVs and ICE vehicles?**

IN THIS UNIT YOU WILL ...

- learn vocabulary for talking about sustainability and performance
- practice language for dealing with international partners
- develop skills for presenting and explaining facts

5 | Sustainability and performance

How does your company deal with sustainability? Place the words into the mind map and then add your own ideas.

develop more environmentally friendly vehicles | meet emission standards | reduce production waste | introduce an employee idea program

```
                    Company Goals        Production
                    & Programs           Resources
_____                              _____
_____          ┌──────────────┐    _____
                 │ Sustainability │
_____          └──────────────┘    _____
_____                              _____
                    Compliance          Products
                    & Regulations       & Materials
```

Compare your answers with a partner and discuss the following questions.

1 What has changed at your job to become more sustainable?
2 How do you view sustainability? Is there anything you do at your workplace to reduce the environmental impact?
3 Do you think it is possible for companies to act sustainably and make a profit? Give reasons.

1 Listen to this podcast about sustainable practices in the automotive industry and fill in the missing words.

06

Sustainable solutions	
Advantages of using sustainable materials: • are renewable • use fewer _____ [1] fuels • production emits fewer _____ [2]	Reduce the impact of battery production: • improve battery technology • _____ [3] batteries • use more _____ [4] energy in production
Create a sustainable supply chain: • optimize logistics • use _____ [5] practices in packaging and transportation	Meet emission regulations and reduce the carbon footprint: • _____ [6] EV sales • use more lightweight materials • recycle materials and _____ [7] components

---

VOCABULARY

to **be delighted** erfreut sein
to **be a gearhead** Benzin im Blut
  haben
carbon-neutral CO2-neutral
to **emit sth** etw. ausstoßen

carbon footprint ökologischer
  Fußabdruck
fossil fuels fossile Brennstoffe
greenhouse gases Treibhausgase

renewable erneuerbar
reusable
  wiederverwendbar
tailpipe Auspuffrohr
ultimately letztendlıch

DID YOU KNOW?

In English there are many words for the German word *"Ziel"*.
• a **goal** or **aim** is used for larger and abstract topics,
  e.g. **company goals**
• a **target** usually refers to specific topics like numbers,
  e.g. **sales targets**
• an **objective** is often used for short-term actions,
  e.g. **meeting objectives**

2 Which of the statements are true? Listen to the dialogue again if necessary.
Then make the false statements true.

True   False

1 Greenmotion uses recycled and natural materials to reduce its environmental impact.
2 Customers think sustainability is more important than the design of a car.
3 The use of natural materials has more than one advantage.
4 Battery production for electric vehicles (EVs) is not very energy-intensive.
5 Renewable energy doesn't help contribute to cleaner solutions.
6 A sustainable supply chain can only be achieved with the help of suppliers.
7 Greenmotion wants the production of its vehicles to be completely carbon neutral.
8 Increasing EV sales is enough to reduce the environmental footprint of Greenmotion.

3 Complete the sentences from the dialogue with the correct form of "to meet" or "to reach".

1 A car has to _____ customer expectations.

2 One step for making a supply chain sustainable is _____ agreements with suppliers.

3 The next milestone Greenmotion wants to _____ is carbon neutral production lines.

4 To _____ future environmental regulations, different solutions are needed.

5 Automakers need to _____ tougher targets for cars on the roads.

6 A company has to _____ a compromise between shareholder obligations and environmental responsibility.

4 Fill in the first column with "reach", "meet" or both. Then add the words from exercise 3 that fall into the same category as the rest of the words in each line, forming collocations with "reach", "meet" or both.

1 _____	goal	aim	_____	objective
2 _____	a compromise	_____	an understanding	a deal
3 _____	a deal	a decision	_____	an agreement
4 _____	_____	emission limits	legal requirements	standards
5 _____	requirement	demand	_____	needs
6 _____	_____	a deadline	the schedule	the timeline

In pairs, ask each other about your work week using at least one collocation from each line.

5 Have you ever heard of OKRs? Read this email and fill in the missing words. Then answer the questions with a partner.

achieve I challenge I fail to meet I objectives I pursue I track

VOCABULARY

ambitious ehrgeizig
to **pursue sth** etw. verfolgen, anstreben
to **track sth** etw. verfolgen

This year we will use _____ [1] and Key Results (OKRs) for our sustainability goals. OKRs are a powerful tool to set and _____ [2] ambitious goals because they offer a clear structure that connects our long-term aims with specific tasks. They present a _____ [3] as they demand commitment and focus, but they are flexible: We can shift our goals if we need to change them or _____ [4] them. The strategy has four levels: The **vision** serves as our inspirational North Star. The **mission** shows how we work towards our vision. **Objectives** define the outcomes needed to _____ [5] each mission statement. **Key results** are short-term, measurable results that _____ [6] progress toward each objective.

1 How do you set and measure goals in your team? Explain to your partner.
2 Do you find the OKR method useful? Do you know of any other methods? Give examples.

6 SIMULATION

Step 1: Create small groups of 3-4 people.

Step 2: Hold a workshop to define more objectives and key results to make the processes and products of Nextron Motors more sustainable. Use the agenda on the right and language from exercises 4 and 5 to help you. Record your results in the chart below.

Step 3: After your meeting, discuss how it went.
- What points of the meeting went well?
- Which areas were difficult?
- What could have helped to make things easier?

Meeting Agenda:
Sustainability Objectives

- Define two more objectives to fulfill the mission statement: "Drive sustainability in processes and products". Objectives are specific.
- Define two key results for each new objective. Key results should be measurable (a number, a percentage or a number range).

Mission: Drive Sustainability in our processes and products		
Objective: Reduce carbon emissions in our value chain	**Objective:**	**Objective:**
Key Results: 1 Work with suppliers to meet our sustainability requirements. 50% of suppliers within one year. 2 Track and report on emissions reduction progress on a quarterly basis.	**Key Results:**	**Key Results:**

7 Listen to a dialogue between Gerhard Schneider und Li Wei and fill in the missing information on Li Wei's notepad.

Current project task: _____

Budget situation: _____

Next major milestone: _____

8 Listen to the call again and fill in the missing information. Then match sentences (1–8) to their function (a–h).

1 Li Wei _____.

2 I am _____ to see how things are progressing.

3 Everything is _____.

4 What is _____ on material sourcing?

5 Now _____ next steps.

6 It _____ this topic face-to-face.

7 Well, I think _____ everything.

8 Thanks _____.

a asking for an update

b closing remarks

c purpose of call

d receiver answering phone

e ending a call

f changing the topic

g suggesting future contact

h giving an update

Additional phrases:

_____

_____

_____

_____

_____

_____

_____

Can you add any other phrases? Write them on the lines above and compare with a partner.

9 Did you use any of the phrases in a recent business call? Which could you have used?

10 **Read this article on cultural intelligence. Then discuss the questions below with a partner.**

Mastering Cultural Intelligence for Global Success

Cultural intelligence focuses on how people from different cultural backgrounds recognize, respect and deal with cultural differences. Intercultural experts have created models to describe different culturally-based attitudes or dimensions. Communication, the building of personal relationships and leadership expectations are some of the differences experts focus on.

One important aspect to remember is that national culture is only one "layer" that may affect how a person acts. Ultimately, it is important not to overlook that we deal with individuals who have their own personality, needs and experiences that shape their behaviour. There is no right or wrong when it comes to work styles. A good approach is to be open-minded and curious. Cultural intelligence is a skill that can be built up over time. It will not only help you and your company collaborate more successfully with international partners, but it can also offer a good chance for learning and personal growth!

---

1 What do you expect from business partners to collaborate effectively? List five characteristics or behaviors that are important to you when working together.

2 Compare your expectations from question 1 with a partner. What is similar? What is different? Where do you think these expectations come from?

3 Have you ever worked in a different team or for a different company? Did you notice any differences in work or leadership styles? Give examples.

4 Do you have any experience working with international partners? Give examples. Look at your five characteristics in question 1 and talk about different expectations international partners might have.

11 **Match the sentence halves. Then put them in the correct order.**

1 How are you, Li? It's great to see you again.

2 Okay, I will speak to my boss. I am

3 Okay we can take a step back and talk about the budget and the goals.

4 Yes, that would help. It would be great to meet face-to-face

5 I will see if this is possible.

6 I realize the milestone is important for you Gerhard,

7 Yes, all fine. In my view the first topic to discuss

8 They are good Gerhard. Thanks for asking.

a confident we can make this project a success!

b and align the project goals with our managers.

c is defining the supplier list to meet the next milestone. What do you think?

d Then we can look at how we work together.

e I hope all is well with yours too.

f If we can't arrange a face-to-face meeting, we can set up a video conference.

g How is the family?

h but it might help to speak about the goals and budget first.

 With a partner, compare the discussion above with the transcript to track 7 on page 68. What is different in Gerhard and Li's communication? Find three differences. What other advice would you give them to improve their communication and collaboration with each other?

12 **Read the following report about the development of electric car sales and complete the sentences below based on the information in the graph. Then create your own sentences.**

The Eight-Year Journey of Electric Cars

Not too long ago, electric cars were rare. In 2016, global sales did not even amount to one million cars. As the technology improved and sustainability became more important, EV sales have risen. Global sales exceeded two million cars in 2018 and the following years saw a sharp increase in sales, showing a growing shift towards electric vehicles as a mainstream option. Despite the global pandemic, in 2021 EV sales doubled from the previous year, due to government support and advancements in technology. The following year the trend continued as around one in seven new cars sold was electric. By 2023 the market share of EVs has increased substantially and nearly 14 million EVs were sold worldwide.

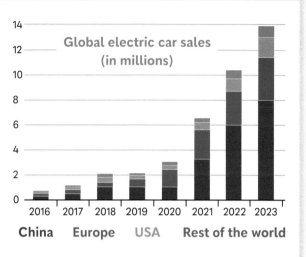

1 Global EV sales since 2020 have _____ .

2 In 2020 sales in Europe _____ .

3 Compared with 2019, the sales in 2023 in the USA _____ .

4 Sales figures in China in 2023 _____ .

5 _____

6 _____

7 _____

In pairs, make comparisons using the information in the graph and the Useful Phrases below.

1 Sales in 2016 and 2017	4 Sales in 2019 and 2023	7 Rest of the world and China
2 Sales in 2018 and 2020	5 Europe and China	8 USA and rest of the world
3 Sales in 2020 and 2022	6 USA and China	9 Europe and rest of the world

---

USEFUL PHRASES   Presenting numbers

Moving up & down
- Sales figures increased by …
- The number rose sharply / substantially by 5% …
- The amount dropped / fell in 2027 due to …
- Sales were higher / lower than …

Remaining stable
- Sales were about / around / approximately …
- The number remained constant at …
- The total amount was just over / under …

Degree of change
- There was a dramatic / sharp increase in …
- In 2018 there was a substantial / significant decrease in …
- There was a small / minor drop in sales …

13 **Fill in the blanks of this financial report.**

achieve | compared to | market share | meet | product portfolio | profitability | reach | supply chain | sustainability

Financial Highlights: The total revenue for the year was 65 billion euros, a 9% increase

_____ [1] last year. This growth is due to our strong sales performance in all markets and

the rising demand for our electric vehicles (EVs). Nextron Motors _____ [2] a net profit of

$ 8.1 billion, which was a 15% increase over the previous year. This growth proves our commitment to

efficiency and cost management. The gross margin for the year was 9.1%, which shows the

_____ [3] of our operations and our ability to manage production costs. Nextron Motors

sold a record-breaking 2.4 million EVs during the year, _____ [4] our sales targets and

showing strong demand for our vehicles. Our global _____ [5] increased to 2.9%, which

shows our growing presence in the worldwide automotive market.

Operational Highlights: We introduced several new models, including the Nextron-Z9 and

Nextron-ZY, which received positive feedback from customers. These additions to our lineup show our

commitment to innovation and to _____ [6] the needs of our customers. Despite

challenges in global _____ [7], we minimized disruptions to production schedules and

delivery timelines. We are also continuing to optimize our processes. Nextron Motors remains

committed to _____ [8] with initiatives such as reducing carbon emissions, promoting

renewable energy sources, and implementing environmentally friendly practices.

Future Outlook: Nextron Motors is well-positioned for continued growth and success. We will continue

to focus on innovation, sustainability and customer-centricity as we expand our _____ [9]

and enter new markets.

14 **Match the English word to the German translation.**

1	profitability	a	Marktanteil
2	gross margin	b	Nettogewinn
3	market share	c	Umsatz
4	net profit	d	Verkaufszahlen
5	revenue	e	Rentabilität
6	vehicle sales	f	Bruttomarge

VOCABULARY

commitment *hier:* Engagement
disruption Störung, Unterbrechung
lineup Produktreihe
need Bedürfnis
operational betrieblich

15 **MEDIATION** ───────────────────────────────────────

With a partner, turn to the Partner Files and follow the instructions on explaining graphs.

▷ Partner Files, File 6: Partner A, pages 56-57 | Partner B, pages 60-61

Driving Sustainability:
The Importance of ESG for Automotive Manufacturers

In today's world, where climate change is a real concern, automotive manufacturers are embracing sustainability like never before. One key concept which measures company performance in terms of sustainability is ESG – Environmental, Social, and Governance criteria. What exactly is ESG, and why should car companies care about it?

Environmental factors refer to how companies interact with nature and their impact on the environment. This includes reducing carbon emissions, conserving resources, and using renewable energy. Social factors focus on how companies treat people, both within and outside their company walls. Are they fostering diversity and inclusion, ensuring workplace safety or supporting local communities? Lastly, governance factors look at the internal workings of companies and topics like transparency, ethics, and accountability.

Does ESG really impact performance? Consumers are increasingly conscious of the environmental and social impact of what they buy and many want to know that their new car isn't contributing to global warming or exploiting workers. Better sales aren't the only financial effect of ESG. A growing trend links ESG performance with the interest rates for loans that banks and financial institutions offer car companies. The better the ESG rating, the lower the interest rate a company receives.

ESG doesn't only have a financial impact. As emissions regulations continue to tighten, it helps companies remain competitive by staying ahead of the curve, dealing with risks and taking advantage of new market opportunities. Whether it's developing electric vehicles, investing in renewable energy solutions or having a more diverse and inclusive workforce, it can help companies become better. ESG, in many ways, is a roadmap for carmakers to navigate towards a more sustainable and socially responsible future!

1 Does the environmental and social performance of a company affect what you buy? Give examples.
2 Is your corporate strategy affected by environmental or social factors? Give examples.
3 What else could be done to make companies more ethical or socially and environmentally conscious?

VOCABULARY

accountability Verantwortung, Haftung
environmentally conscious umweltbewusst
to **exploit so/sth** jmdn./etw. ausbeuten
to **foster sth** etw. fördern
global warming globale Erwärmung
interest rate Zinssatz
loan Darlehen
to **stay ahead of the curve** der Zeit voraus sein
to **tighten sth** etw. verschärfen

IN THIS UNIT YOU WILL ...

- learn vocabulary for car marketing and car-buying attitudes
- acquire language for convincing and persuading
- develop skills for dealing with customers and handling complaints

6 | Sales and marketing

 What do you look for in a car? Take the following survey on car-buying attitudes, adding your own ideas to the list. Compare with a partner and discuss the questions below.

Your ranking (1–12)			Partner's ranking (1–12)
	a	Brand	
	b	Design	
	c	Environmental friendliness	
	d	Fuel consumption	
	e	Interior features	
	f	Performance	
	g	Powertrain	
	h	Price	
	i	Safety	
	j	Size	
	k	_____	
	l	_____	

1 Has your car-buying attitude changed? What was different when you bought your first car?
2 Do you think marketing campaigns really impact car-buying attitudes? Has advertising ever affected something you have bought?
3 What kind of car advertising is most effective (TV, magazines, sports events, social media)? Give reasons.

1 **Are car-buying attitudes changing? Read this blog on car-buying attitudes and marketing strategies and put the correct headline above each paragraph.**

Latest trends in digital marketing | New ways of connecting with customers | The power of video | What factors drive buying decisions? | Why digital marketing works

Changing strategies for a changing market

In the competitive world of automotive sales, carmakers are developing new strategies to meet the changing attitudes and behavior of car buyers.

_____
1

Topics like sustainability, new technologies and convenience are influencing customer attitudes more than ever. With the growing concern for the environment, carmakers are focusing on more eco-friendly electric and hybrid models. Clean energy and a lower carbon footprint are also topics that attract environmentally conscious customers. For consumers living in large cities and urban centers, the convenience of **car subscriptions** and shared mobility services are attractive. Advanced features like interior smart systems and autonomous driving appeal to buyers who like new technologies.

_____
2

Where carmakers are reaching consumers is also changing. Traditional **media channels** like television, print, and radio are still used. More and more carmakers, however, are using digital platforms to reach a wider audience. Companies are investing in **search engine optimization (SEO)** and digital marketing to engage with consumers across multiple **touchpoints**.
Search engine optimization is very cost-effective and advertising on social media platforms allows companies to interact with potential buyers, share engaging content and build brand awareness. Partnerships with social media influencers allow carmakers to promote their brand by reaching a wider audience and building trust with followers.

_____
3

Platforms like YouTube can showcase product features and communicate **brand values** with online ads and virtual test drives. Such engaging content can influence buying decisions in a way traditional advertising cannot.

_____
4

Innovative channels such as virtual reality (VR) and augmented reality (AR) give consumers **immersive experiences** and let them interact with products. VR showrooms and AR-enabled apps allow buyers to explore different models, customize features and visualize their dream car in real-world settings. Such new technologies improve the buying experience and drive **customer engagement**.

_____
5

The shift towards digital marketing reflects a wider trend in society. Online research, social media sharing and interactive content is the new normal. Online marketing lets carmakers tailor their message to specific target audiences to drive **brand loyalty** and car sales. It is quite different from traditional advertising when customer engagement was much more passive!

VOCABULARY

to **appeal to so** _hier:_ jmdm. gefallen
brand value Markenwert
car subscription Fahrzeugabonnement
convenience _hier:_ Verbraucher*innen-
   freundlichkeit
customer engagement Kund*innenbindung
to **showcase sth** etw. zur Schau stellen
search engine optimization (SEO)
   Suchmaschinenoptimierung
showroom Ausstellungsraum
to **tailor sth** etw. maßschneidern
touchpoint Berührungspunkt

2 Add the bold-faced words from the text to the correct definition.

1 _____ : a commitment from a customer to buy from the same company

2 _____ : beliefs a company stands for

3 _____ : a monthly rate paid to use a vehicle

4 _____ : interactions that strengthen the bond between companies and customers

5 _____ : when a person can interact with the environment in a real or imaginary world

6 _____ : outlets where companies can communicate their message to their target audience

7 _____ : moments when companies can interact with customers

8 _____ : improving a website's chances of appearing in online search results

Describe your company's marketing strategy using at least three of the words from above.

 3 Compare with exercise 1 and circle the correct word. In pairs, ask and answer the questions.

1 What kind of advanced features *appeal / adopt* to buyers who like new technologies?
2 What media *values / channels* are still used although digital platforms are more popular?
3 What services do OEMs offer consumers in large cities for more *convenience / touchpoints*?
4 What helps companies engage with consumers across multiple *touchpoints / showrooms*?
5 What allows companies to *show off / showcase* product features and communicate brand values?
6 What do VR *touchpoints / showrooms* and AR-enabled apps allow online shoppers to explore?
7 What helps improve the buying experience and drive customer *engagement / convenience*?
8 Companies can *tailor / showcase* their message to specific target audiences. Why is this a benefit?

 4 Complete the table with the marketing strategies from exercise 1. Then discuss the questions below.

Method	Objectives	Benefits
Search Engine Optimization (**SEO**)	• Improve a website's chances of appearing in online search results	Attracts potential buyers 1
Social Media Marketing (**SMM**)	• Use platforms to connect with audiences	 2
Video Marketing (**VM**)	 3	• Emotional impact influences buyer decisions
Influencer Marketing (**IM**)	 4	• Reach a new, wider audience • Build trust with followers

1 Which of the four methods is the most/least effective? Compare and contrast using the Useful Phrases.
2 How do they compare to traditional methods? When is digital marketing more/less effective?

 USEFUL PHRASES Comparing and contrasting information

- Compared to/with video marketing, influencer marketing is ...
- SMM is just as effective as ...
- SEO is not as effective as ...
- IM is more effective than ...

- While VM impacts buyer decisions, it doesn't ...
- Whereas SEO is cost-effective, it isn't ...
- Although IM reaches a new audience, it isn't ...
- SEO attracts potential buyers, however, it doesn't have the same impact as ...

5 **Part of good marketing and communication is being convincing. Match the sentence halves.**

1 Think of the impact:
2 The figures tell the story.
3 Isn't it time we took action?
4 The current situation clearly shows
5 I understand your view,
6 In the long run,

a We need to invest more in video content now!
b but I know you appreciate that our target group is much younger.
c search engine optimization is more effective than better.
d The new model is a complete success!
e digital marketing works. Sales are up!
f Top performance and eco-friendliness – the new Z9!

6 **Listen to a consultant report on recent marketing campaigns from Nextron Motors' competition and fill in the missing information.**

08

Star Cars: "Galactic Velocity" Campaign

Objective: Position Star Cars as the high-performance car of the future.

Concept: Blend sci-fi look with

_____ [1] technology.

Highlights: Released high-tech teaser videos. Hosted a "galactic" launch event with test drives.

_____ [2] influencers to share exclusive content using #GalacticVelocity.

Social Media Reach: _____ [3] million impressions

Website Visits: 15 million unique visitors.

_____ [4] booked a test drive. 3.3% from website.

Greenmotion: "EcoRevolution" Campaign

Objective: Showcase company commitment to sustainability and electric mobility.

Concept: _____ [5] environmental consciousness with high-performance electric cars.

Highlights: Created a web series on

Greenmotion's _____ [6] manufacturing process. Used digital ads showing zero emissions. Held tree-planting events with ecological groups.

Documentary Views: _____ [7]

Planting: 100,000 trees

Pre-orders: _____ [8] reservations for EXQ

In pairs, compare the campaigns using phrases from exercise 5 and the Useful Phrases on page 48.

1 Which campaign is more convincing? Give reasons.
2 What aspects could be improved? Gather two ideas for each campaign.

USEFUL PHRASES **Convincing and persuading**

Appealing to emotions
• Imagine if we …
• Think about the impact on …
• Look at the success we would have …

Giving reasons and examples
• We have to do this because …
• The most important factor is …
• There are many reasons why it's better. In particular …
• One example why it is …

Using data / facts
• It's a well-known fact that …
• The numbers show …
• Experts agree …

Personal experience
• In my experience …
• I've been in a similar situation before and would …
• Our last project showed that …

7 How convincing are you? In pairs, take turns convincing each other using the Useful Phrases on page 49. Use the methods given in brackets.

1 Show your partner why their next car purchase should/shouldn't be an electric car. (Using data / facts)
2 You need a larger team for your project. (Give reasons and examples)
3 Show why clearer project responsibilities would help your team. (Appealing to emotions)
4 Your team needs more training for an upcoming project. (Personal experience)
5 Your partner wants more project meetings. You disagree. (Give reasons and examples)
6 Your company's sports car model is better than the competition's. (Using data / facts)

8 MEDIATION

Step 1: Create groups of three. You are a member of the marketing team for the Z9 and your task is to come up with a marketing campaign for the launch. Select a role from the Partner Files (File 7):
Partner A, page 57 | Partner B, page 61 | Partner C, page 63

Step 2: After studying your role, hold the meeting using the agenda to the right. Using the Useful Phrases on page 49, each member should make a short convincing proposal of their idea. After the presentations, compare and discuss the proposals using the Useful Phrases on page 48. Decide on the best idea for each of the five topics and record your results.

Step 3: After your meeting discuss how it went.
• What points of the meeting went well?
• Which areas were difficult?
• What could have helped to make things easier?

Z9 Launch Campaign: "Unleash the Future"

1 Digital Marketing
2 Content Creation
3 Advertising and Media
4 Events and Trade Shows
5 Marketing Technology and Software

9 What is customer experience? Add the words from the box to the following customer relationship guideline. Use the vocabulary box on the next page to help you.

acknowledge | empathize | inquiry | request | respond | value

Welcome every interaction:
• _____ [1] customers from the very first touchpoint.
• Engage with a customer quickly.

_____ [2] and understand:
• Put yourself in the customer's shoes. Listen actively and understand their needs.
• Show real empathy, especially during challenging situations.

Collaborate across teams:
• If customers have a technical _____ [3], contact the relevant department.
• Cross-functional teamwork ensures comprehensive solutions.

Act with integrity:
• Assist customers with accurate information.
• _____ [4] when you don't have all the answers.

Resolve efficiently:
• Handle inquiries quickly and set clear expectations for a resolution.
• _____ [5] to inquiries with long-term solutions that benefit both sides.

Ensure consistency:
• Every interaction reflects our brand. Stay professional and positive.
• _____ [6] feedback and adjust when needed.

WE CARE about our customer's experience!

to **acknowledge sth** etw. anerkennen
to **adjust sth** etw. anpassen
to empathize with so mit jmdm. mitfühlen
inquiry Anfrage

to **put oneself in someone's shoes**
  sich in jmds. Lage versetzen
to **request sth** etw. anfordern
resolution Lösung
to **value so** jmdn. wertschätzen

10 Vocabulary building: Fill in the missing forms.

Noun	Verb
assistance	
acknowledgment	
	to empathize
	to inquire
request	
resolution	
response	
value	

11 Replace the underlined word with the correct form of a word from exercise 10. Take turns asking and answering the questions with a partner referring to the guideline in exercise 9.

1 When should you <u>appreciate</u> customers?
2 When is it important to show real <u>understanding</u> for your customer?
3 What should you do when customers have a <u>question</u> about technical topics?
4 Why should you <u>admit</u> you don't have the answer?

5 How should you <u>solve</u> customer inquiries?
6 With what kind of solutions should you <u>answer</u> customer inquiries?
7 What should you always <u>help</u> customers with?
8 What should you <u>ask for</u> at the end of customer contact?

12 Listen to a phone call of a customer complaint about their Z9 and add the missing information to the form. Then answer the questions below with a partner.
09

Name:	Model / Year:	Description of Problem:

Next Steps:

1 _____ 2 _____

1 Have you ever complained about a product or service? Give examples.
2 Were you satisfied with the company's response and resolution of the problem? Give examples.

Look at the guideline in exercise 9 again. How would you rate Alex's performance according to the six topics? What improvements would you suggest?

13 **A car clinic interviews potential customers to help plan future vehicles. Answer the questions.**

1 Would you be interested in a car subscription or mobility service?

2 Is sustainability a top three factor when you decide on a car?

3 Are brand and image important factors when you buy a car?

4 Would you consider paying extra for premium features?

5 Is after sales and customer care important for you?

6 Which design of the three prototypes below do you prefer? Why?

7 When buying a sports car what do you look for? (Select 3)

☐ Performance ☐ Technology ☐ Fuel efficiency

☐ Reputation ☐ Handling ☐ Design

8 What color do you look for?

☐ Racing Red ☐ Pearl White ☐ Metallic Silver

☐ Midnight Black ☐ Electric Blue ☐ Other

9 Is car connectivity (car-to-car, car-to-x) important for you?

10 What infotainment features are important for you?

In pairs, compare your results. What do you agree on and where do you disagree? Rank the questions and select a "top three" that drive buyer behavior.

Ranking: _____ Top Three: _____

14 SIMULATION _____

Step 1: Create groups of three. Your task is to plan the next Nextron Motors sports car. The meeting objective is to reach an agreement on the new car's basic concept.

Step 2: Each person selects a meeting role from the Partner Files (File 8):
Partner A, page 57 | Partner B, page 61 | Partner C, page 63

Step 3: After preparing your role, hold the meeting. Use the agenda to the right to record your results. Each member should make a short 90 second sales pitch about their vision for the new sports car. Discuss the pitches and decide on a design. Then discuss the remaining agenda points individually. Use the Useful Phrases from this unit as well as the results from exercise 13 as part of your discussion.

Step 4: Review how the meeting went.
• What points of the meeting went well?
• Which areas were difficult?
• What could have helped to make things easier?

Nextron Vortex Basic Concept

1 Design

_____

2 Powertrain

_____

3 Exterior features

_____

4 Interior features

_____

5 Brand alignment

_____

6 Marketing message

_____

6 Competition

_____

The future of car sales: Netflix or Amazon? ☰

In the ever-changing world of car sales, two distinct business models we know from our daily lives could redefine how we buy and use cars.

Imagine a world where carmakers directly interact with customers and dealers become "agents" that get a fixed commission for every car they sell. Sounds impossible? The agency model is closer than you think!

Why is it attractive? For car buyers it means they can avoid the "hated" price negotiation. The benefit for carmakers is they can directly interact with customers and get a better understanding of their needs. Data ownership is another factor. Collecting valuable customer data allows carmakers to better target their marketing and personalize offers. As consumers already research and configure cars online, why shouldn't they buy them online too? The seamless online buying experience made popular by platforms like Amazon is nothing new. And there is one more reason: the price. By removing dealership markups, prices become more competitive.

Another trend is challenging a second long held belief – car ownership as a long-term commitment.

The subscription model believes consumers are willing to pay a monthly fee for a car, like they already do for services like Netflix. Why you might ask? Firstly, it means more convenience and no hidden expenses for buyers as car subscriptions cover all costs (maintenance, repairs, insurance, etc.) except fuel. Secondly, it gives consumers total flexibility. A subscriber can swap cars as needed. For a person living in the city it could mean using an electric car during the week and a SUV for a weekend getaway. The last reason is sustainability. Car subscriptions reduce overproduction and waste.

Car buying in the future probably won't offer one model or the other, but a combination of models to best suit the needs of different customers!

1 **Explain the agency model in your own words. Can you see any disadvantages to the model?**

2 **Now describe the car subscription model in your own words. Can you imagine having a car subscription? Why or why not?**

3 **How do you think most people will buy cars in ten years? What kind of advertising will convince potential buyers? What differences in customer experience and customer care will there be?**

VOCABULARY

commission Provision, Gebühr
data ownership Datenbesitz
getaway Ausflug
hidden expenses versteckte Kosten
markup Aufpreis
to swap sth etw. austauschen

Partner A

File 1   UNIT 1   Exercise 6

Step 1: You want to show your boss a presentation on Thursday that is scheduled for Friday. Partner B is a colleague who is going to work on the presentation with you. You start the conversation with Partner B to set a date to meet.
Step 2: Respond to Partner B's request.
Step 3: The Project Milestone Meeting has been postponed until the following week. Inform Partner B.

Your schedule next week:

Monday: Facilitating all-day workshop 9 am – 5 pm
Tuesday: Carrying out tests 9 am – 12 pm
Wednesday: Coordinating project results 10 am – 12 pm, Consulting colleagues in production facility 1 – 3 pm
Thursday: Preparing presentation for Friday 9 am – 12 pm, Meeting with boss 1 – 3 pm
Friday: Project milestone deadline at 9 am

File 2   UNIT 2   Exercise 16

Nextron Motors Development Department:
You receive the following email from your German headquarters before your weekly status meeting with the NextGen Software Development Team. Read it and prepare yourself for the meeting with NextGen Software.

Sehr geehrtes Projektteam,

aufgrund der aktuellen wirtschaftlichen Situation müssen wir das Budget für die Entwicklung der nächsten Softwaregeneration für den Z9-Motor um 30% kürzen. Unser Ziel ist es, so viele Softwarefunktionen wie möglich zu entwickeln, ohne dabei 30% der neuen Funktionen zu verlieren. Ich bin der Ansicht, dass unsere Geschäftspartner*innen effektiver in den täglichen Besprechungen kommunizieren und ihre Aufgaben besser priorisieren könnten. Trotz des aktuellen Budgets von nur 70% hoffen wir, 90% oder sogar 95% der Funktionen entwickeln zu können. Es ist wichtig, diese Änderung transparent an unseren Partner zu kommunizieren, um den Projekterfolg und den Zeitplan nicht zu gefährden.

Bitte setzen Sie sich mit ihnen in Verbindung, um gemeinsam eine Lösung zu finden.

Mit freundlichen Grüßen
T. Haas, Projektleiter Z9 Successor

Meeting facilitator:
You work for an internationally recognized mediation office. Mistakenly your instructions were sent to you in German because it came from Nextron Motors. Read the email and prepare your role.

Sehr geehrte Frau Rodriguez-Schenk,

wir möchten Sie bitten, als Mediatorin eine Verhandlung zu begleiten. Ihr Ziel ist es, eine kooperative Atmosphäre zu schaffen und eine Win-Win-Situation zu erreichen.

Ihre Aufgaben während der Sitzung „Z9 Successor":
- Erläuterung des Zwecks der Sitzung und Vorstellung der Teilnehmer*innen.
- Sicherstellen, dass die Gruppe fokussiert und auf Kurs bleibt.
- Ermutigung der Teilnehmer*innen, ihre Ideen weiter zu erläutern und auf den Ideen anderer aufzubauen.
- Diskussionsleitung durch gezielte Fragen und Aufforderungen zur Entwicklung von Lösungsvorschlägen.
- Gewährleistung einer gleichberechtigten Teilnahme aller Beteiligten.

Die Partnerschaft zwischen den beiden Unternehmen ist wichtig, weshalb eine Lösung gebraucht wird, die beide Seiten berücksichtigt.

Mit freundlichen Grüßen
Christian Ertl, Global Mediation Services

Label the missing parts of the car. If you are not sure, ask Partner B for help by describing where the car part is located. After you have finished, check with Partner B to confirm your answers.

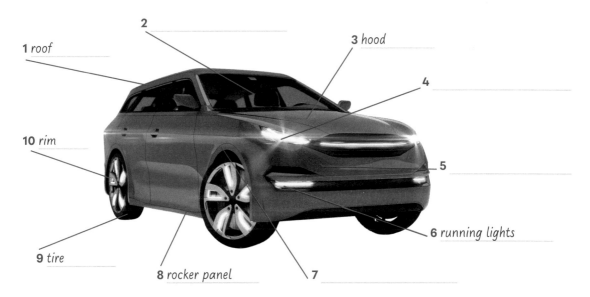

11

12 *side window*

13 *rear window*

14

15 *rear bumper*

16

17 *door handle*

File 5   UNIT 4   Exercise 15

Which part is it?					
Person guessing gets …			Person describing gets …		
(3 points)	(2 points)	(1 point)	(1 point)	(2 points)	
Material	**Joining method**	**Shape**	**Position**	**Possible problems**	**Name of part**
glass and plastic	bonded	rectangular, fragile	on the windshield	cracked	**rear-view mirror**
					rocker panel
					roof
					cupholder
					head rest

File 6   UNIT 5   Exercise 15

Explain the graph on the next page to a partner, using the German text for further details. Your partner should draw the map according to your instructions. Afterwards compare the graph with the original.

Im Jahr 2021 wurde der BWD 10X auf den Markt gebracht und übertraf den Nextron Z9 in Bezug auf Verkaufszahlen und Leistung. Der Nextron Z9 konnte zu Beginn nicht mit dem BWD mithalten.

Trotz des anfänglichen Erfolgs des BWD traten später Qualitätsprobleme auf. Diese führten zu einem dramatischen Rückgang der Verkaufszahlen in den nächsten drei Jahren. Kund*innenbeschwerden über mangelnde Haltbarkeit und technische Mängel beeinträchtigten das Image des BWD.

Im Gegensatz dazu gewann das Z9-Modell an Popularität. Um den Kund*innenanforderungen gerecht zu werden, wurden die Zuverlässigkeit und Leistung des Z9 nach 2023 stetig verbessert. So gelang es dem Nextron Z9 im Jahr 2024 den Markt zu erobern. Dank kontinuierlicher Verbesserungen und einer starken

Marketingkampagne erfreute sich der Z9 wachsender Beliebtheit. Dies führte zu einem Anstieg der Verkaufszahlen. Gegen Ende des Jahrzehnts wird sich der BWD 10X jedoch erholt und zum Z9 aufgeholt haben.

Fazit: Obwohl der BWD 10X im Jahr 2021 den Z9 überflügelte, war sein Absturz aufgrund von Qualitätsproblemen ein schwerwiegender Rückschlag. Der Nextron Z9 nutzte diese Gelegenheit, um sich als zuverlässige Alternative zu etablieren und Marktanteile zurückzugewinnen.

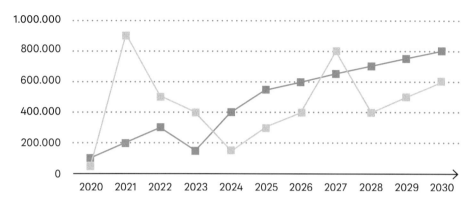

File 7   UNIT 6   Exercise 8

Work together to agree on a launch campaign for the Z9. Due to budget constraints, you only have enough budget for one marketing measure for each of the five topics. Your German colleague, who is a marketing expert, has sent his recommendations. Convince your colleagues these ideas are the best.

- **Digitales Marketing (50% des Budgets): Website-Erstellung und -Optimierung:** Erstellung einer ansprechenden Website für den Z9, einschließlich interaktiver Funktionen und 360-Grad-Ansicht.
- **Inhaltserstellung (20%): Video-Inhalte:** Produktion hochwertiger Videos, die das Design, die Leistung, die Sicherheitsmerkmale und die Benutzererfahrung des Z9 zeigen. Diese Videos können auf der Website, in sozialen Medien und auf YouTube verwendet werden.
- **Werbung & Medien (15%): Print-Anzeigen:** Platzierung ganzseitiger Anzeigen in Automobilzeitschriften und Zeitungen.
- **Veranstaltungen & Messen (10%): Auto-Shows:** Teilnahme an großen Automobilmessen mit Stand mit interaktiven Displays und einem immersiven Erlebnis.
- **Marketingtechnologie & Software (5%): Marketing-Automatisierungstools:** Investition in Software, um E-Mail-Kampagnen und die Segmentierung von Kund*innen zu automatisieren.

File 8   UNIT 6   Exercise 14

You prefer that the new model blends sustainability and elegance.
Sustainability: The new model should use a sustainable supply chain, reduce environmental impact, and have a zero emissions strategy in manufacturing.
Powertrain: full-electric
Materials: lightweight, eco-friendly materials vegan leather, bamboo
Design: sleek lines, futuristic appeal
Interior features: High-tech interior that creates a

seamless natural interior blend of form and function. Cutting-edge safety systems.
Brand alignment: Position model as a gamechanger. Appeal to trend-setters.
Marketing campaign: "Drive Change" Zero emissions, infinite thrills. A documentary-style launch event highlighting the eco-friendly features.

Partner B

File 1   UNIT 1   Exercise 6 ────────────────────────────────────

Step 1: With your colleague (Partner A), you are working on a presentation that is scheduled for Friday, however you have to meet a deadline for another project on Tuesday, which is more important to you than the presentation. Consequently, you prefer to meet on Thursday. Partner A starts the conversation.
Step 2: You suddenly remember your boss needs you at the time you agreed to meet Partner A. Reschedule.
Step 3: Respond to Partner A's information.

Your schedule next week:

Monday:	Team meeting 9 am – 12 pm, Meeting new supplier 1 – 4 pm
Tuesday:	Writing meeting minutes 8 – 10 am, Preparing presentation for other project 1 – 5 pm (Need to meet the 5 pm deadline!)
Wednesday:	Taking a day-off
Thursday:	Reviewing test results with supplier 9 am -12 pm, Participating in taskforce meeting 3 – 5 pm
Friday:	Participating in IT training 9 am – 12 pm

File 2   UNIT 2   Exercise 16 ────────────────────────────────────

NextGen Software Development Department:
You receive the following email from a German manager who works closely with Nextron Motors at their German headquarters. Read it and prepare yourself for the meeting with Nextron Motors.

Liebes Team,

Nextron Motors plant eine Budgetkürzung für unser Projekt, obwohl wir einen Rahmenvertrag unterzeichnet haben. Dies legt eine gewisse Verbindlichkeit fest, doch sollten wir in Anbetracht einer langfristigen Partnerschaft versuchen, eine Win-Win-Lösung zu finden. Zwar sollte sich eine Kürzung des Budgets in weniger Software-Funktionen widerspiegeln, doch könnte dies auch zu Qualitätsproblemen führen, wenn wir beispielsweise versuchen würden, 90% der Funktionen mit nur 70% des Budgets zu liefern. Wir sollten zudem die Teamauslastung überdenken, z.B. weniger Stunden pro Woche für einen kürzeren Zeitraum oder eine verkürzte Arbeitswoche.

Ich wünsche viel Erfolg bei den anstehenden Verhandlungen und stehe bei Fragen zur Verfügung.

Mit besten Grüßen
A. Mueller
Key Account Manager Deutschland, NextGen Software

CEO of supplier "Sealtex":
Sealtex Group Headquarters in Germany sent you this email before your negotiation with Nextron Motors to prepare you.

Sehr geehrter Herr Martínez,

ich hoffe, Sie hatten ein angenehmes Wochenende.

Wir bitten Sie, die bevorstehenden Verhandlungen mit Nextron Motors mit Sensibilität zu führen.
Hier einige wichtige Punkte für die Verhandlung:
Unser Ziel ist es, eine Lösung zu finden, die für beide Seiten vorteilhaft ist. Es sind Änderungen an den Zeichnungen notwendig, und im besten Fall sollen diese Änderungen bezahlt werden. Die Wahrung unserer Geschäftsbeziehungen mit Nextron Motors ist von größter Bedeutung, besonders da eine größere Ausschreibung bevorsteht, bei der wir gute Chancen haben möchten.

Wir vertrauen darauf, dass Sie Sealtex als verlässlichen Partner für Nextron Motors darstellen können. Eine erfolgreiche Verhandlung könnte sich positiv auf Ihre berufliche Zukunft auswirken, möglicherweise mit einer Beförderung zum Hauptsitz der Sealtex-Gruppe in Deutschland.

Mit freundlichen Grüßen
Horst Schmid, Sealtex Group Headquarters

Label the missing parts of the car. If you are not sure, ask Partner A for help by describing where the car part is located. After you have finished, check with Partner A to confirm your answers.

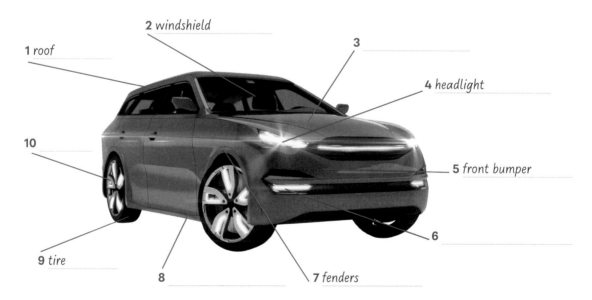

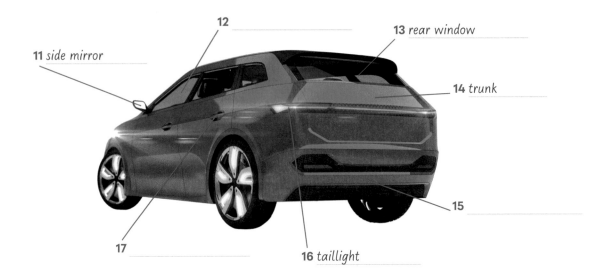

11 *side mirror*
12
13 *rear window*
14 *trunk*
15
16 *taillight*
17

File 5   UNIT 4   Exercise 15

Which part is it?					
Person guessing gets ...			Person describing gets ...		
(3 points)	(2 points)	(1 point)	(1 point)	(2 points)	
Material	**Joining method**	**Shape**	**Position**	**Possible problems**	**Name of part**
plastic	screwed to dashboard	rectangular, stiff	interior, near the dashboard	it won't close	**glove compartment**
					door
					tailgate
					side mirror
					bumper

File 6   UNIT 5   Exercise 15

Explain the graph on the next page to a partner, using the German text for further details. Your partner should draw the map according to your instructions. Afterwards compare the graph with the original.

In den Kund*innenbewertungen des Automagazins Gearhead schnitten die Marken Nextron Motors und Star Cars im Vergleich unterschiedlich ab. Im Jahr 2020 starteten beide Marken auf einem ähnlichen Niveau, doch erwies sich Nextron Motors aufgrund seiner Nachhaltigkeitsstrategie und seines Engagements für die Umwelt als zuverlässigerer Performer.

Hierbei setze Nextron Motors auf umweltfreundliche Technologien und erarbeitete sich einen Ruf als nachhaltige Marke. Die Kund*innen schätzen die Langlebigkeit der Batterien, die Effizienz der Elektromotoren und die geringen Emissionen. Die Marke hat sich als umweltbewusst positioniert und konsequent an ihrer Nachhaltigkeitsagenda festgehalten.

Star Cars hingegen machte zwar ebenfalls Fortschritte, doch gibt es Bedenken, ob sie in den kommenden Jahren an Boden gewinnen können. Das Jahr 2026 wird voraussichtlich ein Wendepunkt sein und Expert*innen gehen davon aus, dass Star Cars gegen Ende des Jahrzehnts an Bedeutung gewinnen wird. Insgesamt ist Nextron Motors derzeit die nachhaltigere Wahl, aber die Zukunft bleibt spannend, da sich die Dynamik im Automobilsektor ständig ändert.

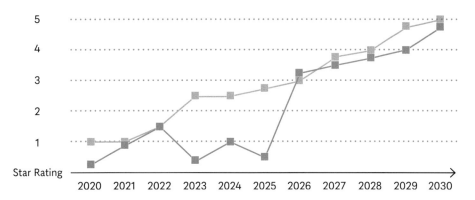

File 7   UNIT 6   Exercise 8 ───────────────────────────────

Work together to agree on a launch campaign for the Z9. Due to constraints, you only have enough budget for one marketing measure for each of the five topics. Your German colleague, who is a marketing expert, has sent his recommendations. Convince your colleagues these ideas are the best.

- **Digitales Marketing (50% des Budgets): Suchmaschinenmarketing:** Investition in Suchanzeigen (Google Ads), um die Sichtbarkeit zu erhöhen, wenn potenzielle Käufer*innen nach verwandten Begriffen suchen.
- **Inhaltserstellung (20%): Blog-Beiträge:** Regelmäßige Veröffentlichung von Blog-Artikeln über die Funktionen, Technologie und Nutzer*innenerfahrungen des Z9. Optimieren der SEO, um Traffic anzuziehen.
- **Werbung & Medien (15%): Fernsehwerbung:** Erstellung emotionaler Anzeigen, die die Einzigartigkeit des Z9 zeigen.
- **Veranstaltungen & Messen (10% des Budgets): Händler-Launch-Veranstaltungen:** Organisation von exklusiven Events für potenzielle Käufer*innen in Z9-Autohäusern. Angebot von Probefahrten, Getränken und persönlicher Beratung.
- **Marketingtechnologie & Software (5% des Budgets): Analysen:** Verwendung von Tools wie Google Analytics, um die Leistung der Kampagnen, das Nutzer*innenverhalten und die Konversionsraten zu verfolgen.

File 8   UNIT 6   Exercise 14 ───────────────────────────────

You prefer that the new model is the last great Internal Combustion Engine (ICE).
Performance: The new model should emphasize raw power, acceleration, and driving dynamics. The car is a tribute to the classic ICE era and should deliver a powerful experience.
Powertrain: 450 hp V-8 gasoline engine
Features: Interior is retro yet luxurious, but

sporty. Sports bucket seats, analog gauges, but high-tech touches. The engine, transmission, and four exhaust pipes appeal to gearheads! Loud and powerful!
Design: aggressive styling and sporty lines
Brand alignment: Show brand as more than just another EV producer.
Marketing campaign: "Old School": Old video clips of classic cars from the history of high performance cars. Position the Vortex as the last great muscle car. Massive Print and TV campaign.

Partner C

File 3   UNIT 3   Exercise 18

Procurement Department "Nextron Motors":
You receive the email below from your business division leader before your meeting with Sealtex.

Sehr geehrte*r Kolleg*in,

als Bereichsleiterin des Einkaufs möchte ich Ihnen einige wichtige Informationen für die bevorstehende Verhandlung mit Sealtex geben.

Unser oberstes Ziel ist es, eine Zusage zu erhalten, dass das Problem gelöst wird und die Meilensteine eingehalten werden, um unsere SOP nicht zu gefährden. Gleichzeitig ist unsere Beziehung zu Sealtex von großer Bedeutung, da andere Lieferanten für Dichtungen finanzielle Schwierigkeiten haben und wir in Zukunft noch stärker auf Sealtex angewiesen sein könnten.

Unser Ziel sollte sein, möglichst wenig für die Änderungen zu zahlen, doch sollte dies auch nicht ausgeschlossen werden.

Mit freundlichen Grüßen
Dr. M. Weiß, Bereichsleiterin Neue Anläufe

File 5   UNIT 4   Exercise 15

Which part is it?					
Person guessing gets ...			Person describing gets ...		
(3 points)	(2 points)	(1 point)	(1 point)	(2 points)	
Material	Joining method	Shape	Position	Possible problems	Name of part
plastic	bonded	depends on brand, light weight	hood	broken	badge
					steering wheel
					infotainment system
					brake pedal
					headlight

Work together to agree on a launch campaign for the Z9. Due to constraints, you only have enough budget for one marketing measure for each of the five topics. Your German colleague, who is a marketing expert, has sent his recommendations. Convince your colleagues these are the best ideas.

- **Digitales Marketing (50% des Budgets)**:
  Social-Media-Werbung: Gezielte Anzeigen auf Plattformen wie Facebook, Instagram und X, um die richtige Zielgruppe zu erreichen.
- **Inhaltserstellung (20%)**:
  Infografiken: Erstellung von Infografiken, die wichtige Verkaufsargumente hervorheben, wie beispielsweise Sicherheitsbewertungen und Konnektivitätsfunktionen sowie die Leistung im Langstreckenbetrieb.
- **Werbung & Medien (15%)**:
  Online-Anzeigen: Investition in Bannerwerbung auf Automobilwebsites und Foren.
  Radio: Radiowerbung auf beliebten Sendern mit Fokus auf die herausragendsten Merkmale des Z9.
- **Veranstaltungen & Messen (10%)**:
  Lokale Veranstaltungen: Sponsoring lokaler Sportveranstaltungen, um mit Kund*innen in Kontakt zu treten und den Z9 zu präsentieren.
- **Marketingtechnologie & Software (5%)**:
  CRM-System: Implementation eines Kund*innenbeziehungsmanagement-System, um potenzielle Kund*innen zu verwalten und Interaktionen zu verfolgen.

You prefer that the new model blends both worlds and sustainability and powerful elegance.
Powertrain: hybrid
Design: rounded sleek lines roadster look
Exterior features: LED Lighting: Diamond-like LED headlights and taillights, minimalist front grille, flush door handles that pop out when needed, carbon fibre sections.

Interior features: Soft leather, aluminum, titanium and premium graphite look in the cockpit. Modern digital controls and touch screen. High-tech features car-to-car connectivity and state of the art infotainment.
Brand alignment: Position brand as both sustainable and sporty. The smart choice.
Marketing campaign: "Electrify Your Senses":
Short, mysterious videos hinting at a hybrid sports car. Social media platforms with teaser videos, countdowns, and behind-the-scenes content. Encourage users to create own content using #ElectrifyYourSenses

Partner D

File 3   UNIT 3   Exercise 18

Development engineer "Nextron Motors":
You receive the email below from a project manager for the Z9 before your meeting with Sealtex.

Liebes Projektmitglied,

ich hoffe, Sie hatten ein schönes Wochenende und einen angenehmen Wochenstart.

Unser oberstes Ziel für diesen Termin ist die Behebung des Problems und die Einhaltung des Projektzeit-plans. Dabei ist es entscheidend, dass unsere SOP nicht gefährdet wird. Wir sind uns bewusst, dass der Lieferant nicht zu 100% verantwortlich ist. Unser Ziel ist es, eine positive Arbeitsatmosphäre zu erhalten, da Sealtex für uns ein strategisch wichtiger Partner ist und unsere anderen Dichtungslieferanten finanzielle Schwierigkeiten haben. Bitte kooperieren Sie mit unserer Einkaufsabteilung in diesem Termin.

Ich bin zuversichtlich, dass wir eine Lösung finden können, die für alle Seiten zufriedenstellend ist.

Mit freundlichen Grüßen
T. Haas, Projektmanager Z9-Nachfolger

File 5   UNIT 4   Exercise 15

Which part is it?					
Person guessing gets …			Person describing gets …		
(3 points)	(2 points)	(1 point)	(1 point)	(2 points)	
Material	**Joining method**	**Shape**	**Position**	**Possible problems**	**Name of part**
plastic	screwed on	round, light weight	back of the car	it can get lost	**gas cap**
					fender
					sun visor
					dashboard
					clutch

TRANSCRIPTS

UNIT 1   Exercise 1 ───────────

 02

1

Mauro: Thanks for coming to our production facility Petra.

Petra: Of course! You really have to look at processes from end-to-end to find all the bottlenecks.

Mauro: Now I just need to find the right solutions!

Petra: I'll prepare a report with my recommendations and send it to you next week.

Mauro: Excellent. Thanks again for consulting us, you've been a real help!

Petra: My pleasure!

2

Brian: I hope you didn't have any trouble finding our office?

Xīn: No, I was given excellent directions at the gate.

Brian: Great. Thanks for sending us the new design last week. The improvements look good.

Xīn: We worked closely with your team on it. I think we are on the right track.

Brian: Come, let me show you to the conference room. Some of my colleagues are also participating in the meeting. They have already carried out tests on the new design and are presenting their results.

Xīn: I'm really interested in hearing their feedback!

3

Andreas: Just give me a thumbs up if you can hear me. ... Thanks! I'd like to introduce Javier. He is taking on some of the day-to-day work in the project.

Javier: I'm looking forward to working with you all!

Andreas: One of Javier's main tasks will be to coordinate project workflows.

Javier: That's right, Andreas. I am setting up a monthly workshop series with all the sub-projects so we keep each other informed of new developments. The workshops should also help us meet our project milestones.

Andreas: Does anyone have any questions for Javier? Marta, I see you've raised your virtual hand. Go ahead.

4

Ankit: Excuse me ... Do you know what time the session on autonomous driving begins?

Hélène: Let me check my program. It's next. Shall we go together?

Ankit: Sure! I'm interested in hearing the latest developments.

Hélène: Do you work on autonomous driving at your job?

Ankit: Not directly. I work in the development department and deal with government authorities.

I make sure our cars meet the technical requirements of each market. What about you?

Hélène: I'm in sales. I work closely with fleet customers and coordinate their needs to the production department.

5

Rita: We need to discuss the timeline for the market launch. We are really behind schedule.

Jens: Should I put that as a topic on our weekly meeting agenda?

Rita: No, I think we need more time. Let's set up a workshop when we get back from this business trip.

Jens: We've still got a few minutes before our flight leaves. I could check everyone's schedules right now. Let's see ... Next Tuesday at 3pm seems to work – except for you. You have a scheduling conflict.

Rita: Next Tuesday at 3? I'll check. That works, I can reschedule my other meeting. Can you please ask John to facilitate the workshop?

Jens: Of course.

UNIT 2   Exercise 1 ───────────

 03

Gerhart: Hi David, hi Anna. We have the results from yesterday's wind tunnel tests. Unfortunately, both the drag and lift coefficients are too high. We need to find a solution with the boundary conditions we have.

David: That's not easy, Gerhart.

Gerhart: What if we looked at the hood?

Anna: The hood design is a crucial element of our design language. Altering it compromises everything else: the grille, the fenders, the angle of the windshield, you name it.

Gerhart: How about lowering the spoiler? Say by 10 millimeters?

Anna: No, if we did that we would lose the sleek line.

Gerhart: We need to find a compromise somewhere ...

Anna: What about lowering the roofline? I was against raising it in the first place. We could still maintain a sleek line with a lower roofline.

David: No, we already have an agreement with the interior design team. They needed to increase the headroom and wanted the cabin to be more spacious.

Gerhart: ... and with a skateboard platform. The cabin already sits high.

Anna: You are right. We don't have much leeway with the cabin.

David: What if we lowered the spoiler by just 5 millimeters and thus made the car longer by 5 millimeters?

Gerhart: Yes, that could work. But extending the rear bumper might make the car too long for the C-segment.

Anna: Those segment classifications are not really exact anyway. Cars change. Nearly every successor is longer than its predecessor.

David: Anna is right! I don't think 5 millimeters is going to affect the segment classification. And interior design won't have a problem because it doesn't impact the cabin.

Gerhart: We are already a few millimeters longer than the current model.

David: I think it is a good compromise.

Gerhart: I'll tell you what. I'll run some simulations to see how it works with the other parameters. It's probably our best option.

David: It might be our only option. The timeline is very tight. The design freeze is next week.

Gerhart: Well, if we can get this issue solved, I think we can meet the next milestone. To be on the safe side, I have already got a plan how to save some time during the development phase. So, I'll check the feasibility of this solution and get back to you as soon as I have the results!

UNIT 3   Exercise 2

 04

Good morning, it's great to be here. I am Sébastien Leroi from the Procurement Department. The purpose of today's talk is to explain our approach for identifying, evaluating, and selecting suppliers. First, I'll talk about the steps needed to receive supplier proposals, next, your role as product owner in the evaluation phase and finally I'll outline the steps once the procurement department receives the evaluation. Afterwards you should have a clear overview of the phases of the supplier selection process and a deeper understanding of your role as product owner. As I'm only talking for five minutes, I'd be happy to answer any questions at the end.

To start with, as a product owner, company policy requires you to outline the standards, expectations, and requirements for the products or services in a specification manual. The specification manual is part of the Request for Proposal or RFP that is distributed to potential suppliers inviting them to submit proposals. You needn't write the RFP yourself, much of it is a standard document.

After the submission phase, the offers must be evaluated. In the evaluation phase you are permitted to conduct questionnaires, site visits, and reference checks to make a complete evaluation. There are three specific tasks you have to fulfil as a product

owner:

1. Comprehensive Understanding: You need to make sure all offers have been understood and are aligned with the technical requirements.

2. Objective Evaluation: You are obliged to assess each proposal fairly and only based on its technical merits. You may not use costs as a decision-making criteria.

3. Document Findings: Internal regulations require you clearly document evaluations so transparency is ensured.

Let's turn to the negotiation phase. This is where we in the procurement department take the lead. We conduct negotiations with suppliers whose offers satisfy all technical requirements. Our goal is to finalize terms, conditions, and pricing. After this, there is the awarding of the contract. The last step is the onboarding. Although there is no formal onboarding process, a list of recommendations should be followed to help ensure a quick and smooth work integration.

In summary, our Supplier Selection Process is a strategic and structured journey of seven major phases, where each step contributes to identifying the most suitable and qualified suppliers. I'd be happy to take your questions now!

UNIT 4   Exercise 1

 05

The 8 Wastes of Lean

As we know processes can be inefficient due to three main factors: "muri", when processes overburden employees or the equipment, "mura" when a process does not flow evenly and "muda" when there is waste in the process. Now, I'd like to take a deep dive into muda and explain the eight different types of waste. I'll also show you how these principles can identify waste in office environments.

The first waste is perhaps the most expensive kind of waste: defects. In production defects can lead to having to scrap parts or rework them, which all mean more costs. In the office defects or poor quality often result from work processes that are not standardized and stable.

Overproduction is the second type. This means producing more than customers demand, which can lead to higher inventory costs and less financial flexibility. One knock-on effect from overproduction on the shop floor could be having to rework more products if quality issues come up. In the office this could be making too many copies or creating lists or reports no one reads.

The next waste is waiting. This basically means any step that slows down a process or creates a bottleneck. There are many examples in office work, like long response times for emails, ineffective meetings or decisions that take too long.

In the original Toyota Production System, Taiichi Ohno outlined seven different types of waste, nowadays most experts have added another waste: not-utilized talent. A typical example in the office as well as on the shop floor, is not giving employees proper training or tasks not suitable for their skill level. It also includes not asking employees for their ideas for how to cut waste in their own work areas, which is potentially the biggest waste of all.

The fifth type of waste is transportation, which is any extra movement of equipment or people that doesn't add value. In production processes, this can result in more work, a higher cycle time and more machine wear and tear. An office example is when colleagues who often work together don't sit near each other.

Inventory is the next waste. In manufacturing this type of waste can include the costs to stockpile materials, work in progress or even finished products. In an office it could be files waiting to be worked on and unused or out-of-date files.

The seventh type is motion. This means removing unnecessary employee movement. On the shop floor, for example, machine operators need their tools close at hand. Office time could be wasted having to search for files or making too many mouse clicks to find them.

The final type is extra processing. This includes anything that exceeds what the process and product requires. Using equipment or materials more expensive than needed or making products with more features than customers require means higher costs. An office example might be preparing a detailed presentation when a one-page summary is enough. Two employees doing the same task is another example.

As you can see with these eight principles there is a lot of potential to reduce waste on the production line and in the office!

UNIT 5 Exercise 1

🔊 06

Host: Welcome to the AutoGear podcast: Where horsepower meets brainpower. I'm your host, Max Gearhead, and today, we're going to discuss all things sustainable in the automotive industry. We have a special guest with us – Dr. Emily Rivers, an environmental expert from Greenmotion, a new player in the automotive sector. Welcome, Emily!

Expert: Thank you, Max! I'm delighted to be here.

Host: Great. I suppose the best place to begin with is the materials needed to build cars. How is Greenmotion sourcing their materials?

Expert: Absolutely, Max. Greenmotion is looking at alternatives to traditional materials. We are using more recycled plastics and biological materials to reduce our carbon footprint. Another topic is using parts made from natural materials like bamboo and vegan leather. The advantages of such materials are clear: they are renewable, use fewer fossil fuels and the production process emits fewer greenhouse gases. Small changes like these add up.

Host: Some traditional materials can't be replaced. Take, for instance, the topic of battery production. How is Greenmotion planning to meet this challenge?

Expert: Great question, Max. Electric vehicles (EVs) are often viewed as a greener alternative, but the production of EV batteries is energy-intensive. We are working on improving battery technology, recycling batteries and using more renewable energy in production.

Host: Interesting! How is Greenmotion working on cleaner solutions beyond batteries?

Expert: One step is creating a sustainable supply chain from start to finish. This means reaching agreements with suppliers to optimize logistics and use greener practices in packaging and transportation. The next milestone we want to meet soon is to make our production lines completely carbon neutral.

Host: How do you plan to meet emission targets for cars on the roads? They are getting tougher and tougher.

Expert: Promoting EV sales can play a big role in reaching that target.

Host: Is that the solution? More EVs on the roads?

Expert: It helps. But we can't meet all future regulations by lowering tailpipe emissions. We need different solutions in how we produce, the materials we use and how we recycle and reuse those materials.

Host: So, it looks like we have kind of come full circle and are back where we started: using renewable or reusable materials!

Expert: That is how it works, Max. Producing sustainably is a circle: from sourcing, to producing, to recycling those materials for the next generation of vehicles. Ultimately, a company like Greenmotion has to reach a compromise between meeting obligations to shareholders and being environ-mentally responsible!

Host: Well, it looks like we have reached the end of another episode of AutoGear. I want to thank Dr. Emily Rivers from Greenmotion for coming. Until next week!

UNIT 5   Exercise 7

🔊 07

Li Wei: Li Wei speaking.
Gerhard Schneider: Hello, this is Gerhard.
Li Wei: Ah yes, Gerhard how are you?
Gerhard Schneider: Good, good. I am just calling to see how things are progressing with our project.
Li Wei: Oh. Yes, everything is on track.
Gerhard Schneider: Did you get my email?
Li Wei: Oh, yes, your email. I saw it. Very detailed.
Gerhard Schneider: What is the latest on material sourcing? Have you reviewed the environmental certifications of our suppliers?
Li Wei: Things are progressing. We have created a list of potential suppliers.
Gerhard Schneider: We don't need a list of suppliers. We need to name which suppliers meet our sustainability criteria.
Li Wei: Of course, Gerhard. We're exploring options. Some suppliers align better than others.
Gerhard Schneider: Yes, good, but we obviously need to meet the deadline in three weeks. We don't really have the time to consider different options.
Li Wei: The project goals are very challenging. We still need some time. I need to align this with my manager.
Gerhard Schneider: We have discussed the project goals before. You need to trust me on this.
Li Wei: Yes, I understand. Something unexpected came up. Are we more flexible on the budget?
Gerhard Schneider: The budget situation has stayed the same. We couldn't increase it.
Li Wei: Oh this will make it very difficult to find the right suppliers.
Gerhard Schneider: But we agreed that the budget was enough. Now, let's talk next steps and milestones. We should be able to enter the construction release next month.
Li Wei: Yes, the construction release. Are you coming on a business trip soon? It could be good to talk about this topic face-to-face.
Gerhard Schneider: No, I have no plans. Well, okay I think that covers everything. Don't forget the deadline is in three weeks.
Li Wei: Yes. Let's see how it goes. Thanks for calling.

UNIT 6   Exercise 6

🔊 08

Good afternoon, everyone. I'm Kate Reynolds from Marketing Pro Consultants. I'm excited to share with you some insights from two recent campaigns in the automotive industry.

First, let's look at Star Cars' "Galactic Velocity" campaign. The objective was to position Star Cars as the high-performance car of the future. They blended sci-fi aesthetics with cutting-edge technology. The campaign included teaser videos, a galactic-themed launch event with test drives, and engagement with influencers who shared exclusive content using the hashtag #GalacticVelocity. The results were impressive: 10 million social media impressions, 15 million unique website visitors, and 500,000 test drive bookings, with 3.3% of website visitors booking a test drive.

Next, we have Greenmotion's "EcoRevolution" campaign. Their objective was to showcase the company's commitment to sustainability and electric mobility. The concept was to merge eco-consciousness with high-performance electric cars. The campaign highlights included a web series on Greenmotion's eco-friendly manufacturing process, partnerships with environmental groups for tree-planting events, and digital ads showcasing zero emissions and long-range capabilities. The results were equally impressive: 6 million views for the documentary, 100,000 trees planted, 300,000 reservations for the EXQ model.

I hope these campaigns provide valuable insights for your work here at Nextron Motors. I'd be happy to answer any questions you have about the campaigns and to help you apply these learnings to your upcoming marketing initiatives. Thank you.

🔊 09

Alex: Good afternoon, my name is Alex. How can I assist you today?

Mr. Rant: Finally! I have been waiting for over an hour on this hotline!

Alex: Yes well. Now I am here. Could I please have your name, sir?

Mr. Rant: My name? It's Rant. R-A-N-T.

Alex: Yes Mr. Rant. How can I help you?

Mr. Rant: I have an issue with the steering wheel of my Z9. Again.

Alex: I am sorry to hear that. And I do apologize for that. Could you kindly provide me with the year of your Z9?

Mr. Rant: It's a 2024. As I said the steering column rattles and sticks when I'm making a simple turn. This is the second time I've had this problem.

Alex: Yes I got that, Mr. Rant. I understand your frustration. Can you describe the specific symptoms? Is the steering suddenly locking in place, or are you experiencing power steering failures?

Mr. Rant: I experience it failing every time I take a curve! The steering wheel gets stiff and I can hardly turn it. It's the second time this month!

Alex: Yes I understand. And I appreciate your patience, Mr. Rant. I just need to ask a few more questions so we can find a quick resolution. Some other Z9 owners have reported similar issues. One owner mentioned the steering failing with a "power steering reduced" warning lamp. Did you receive this warning lamp?

Mr. Rant: I don't think the car is safe to drive to be honest. I need it fixed and fixed properly.

Alex: Of course. I was going to suggest we schedule a service appointment within the next 24 hours.

Mr. Rant: That is a start. But that will mean I will again be without a car.

Alex: We will arrange a courtesy car for you so you will be mobile. I will get back to you within 24 hours with an appointment to pick up your car and bring a courtesy car.

Mr. Rant: Okay. Sounds good.

Alex: Safety is our priority, Mr. Rant. We'll get this sorted out!

Mr. Rant: Okay, bye.

ANSWER KEY

UNIT 1

Exercise 1
Dialogue 1: production facility
Dialogue 2: office building
Dialogue 3: online project meeting
Dialogue 4: automotive conference
Dialogue 5: business trip

Exercise 2
1 recommendations   2 right track   3 workflows
4 milestones   5 requirements   6 fleet customers
7 behind schedule   8 scheduling conflict

Exercise 3
1 e   2 g   3 b   4 h   5 f   6 c   7 a   8 d

Exercise 5
1 invitation; recommendation; to prepare;
to participate; coordination; to improve; to facilitate

Exercise 7
1 open plan office   2 test bench   3 proving grounds
4 closed office   5 shop floor, 6 working from home
7 warehouse, 8 cubicle   9 sales floor

Exercise 10
Topic 1: Electrification
Topic 2: Car Features of the Future
Topic 3: Global Strategy
Topic 4: Trends in Human Resource
Topic 5: New Technologies

Exercise 11
1 false   2 false   3 true   4 true   5 true   6 true
7 true   8 false

Exercise 12
1 advanced   2 to impact   3 to be at risk   4 gains
5 appealing   6 artificial

Exercise 13
1 f   2 e   3 h   4 g   5 d   6 c   7 a   8 b

Exercise 16
Certain: I'm absolutely sure, I'm convinced
Probable: It's likely, I'm confident
Possible: It may be that, There's a chance that
Unlikely: I doubt, It's improbable

UNIT 2

Exercise 1
1 both   2 compromises   3 headroom   4 five
5 classification   6 longer   7 parameters   8 tight
9 development

Exercise 2
1 g   2 e   3 h   4 a   5 c   6 b   7 d   8 f

Exercise 3
Exterior design features: shoulder line, fenders,
grille, headlights, roofline, taillights, windscreen
angle

Interior design features: acoustics, dashboard,
ergonomics, headroom, HMI (human machine
interface), spaciousness, user experience (UX)

Exercise 4
1 station wagon (AE) / estate car (BE)   2 sports car
3 SUV   4 convertible   5 minivan (AE) / MPV (BE)
6 sub-compact   7 sedan / saloon   8 coupe
9 crossover

Exercise 5
1 e   2 f   3 a   4 h   5 b   6 g   7 d   8 c

Exercise 6
exterior design: sleek, boxy
Interior design: spacious, compact
handling: responsive, sluggish
ride: noisy, quiet
drive system: front-wheel, rear-wheel

Exercise 7
3 a concept freeze
9 b construction release
6 c virtual validation
4 d design freeze
7 e purchasing release
5 f system release
10 g production trial
2 h concept phase
8 l part and vehicle testing
1 j customer phase

Exercise 8
1 false   2 true   3 true   4 false   5 false   6 true
7 false   8 true

Exercise 9
to confirm, equipment, to fulfill, purchase,
to release, requirement, specification, to validate

Exercise 10
1 confirms   2 fulfill   3 equipment   4 specification
5 purchasing   6 release   7 requirements   8 validate

Exercise 12
1 capture   2 delegating   3 mitigate   4 objectives
5 deliverables   6 prioritize   7 contingency plan
8 secure

Exercise 13
1 h   2 f   3 g   4 b   5 c   6 a   7 d   8 e

UNIT 3 _____

Warm-up
1 vendor   2 supplier   3 service provider

Exercise 1
1 approach   2 specification manual   3 request for
proposal   4 negotiation   5 terms and conditions
6 onboarding process

Exercise 2
Topic: John's notes
Preparing documents: Oliver's notes
Evaluating suppliers: John's notes
Product owner tasks: Oliver's notes
Negotiating / Onboarding: Oliver's notes

Exercise 3
4 a Presentation structure
6 b Time/question policy
1 c Welcoming participants
2 d Speaker introduction
3 e Goal of presentation
5 f Audience benefit

Exercise 4
1 f   2 c   3 b   4 e   5 d   6 a

Exercise 6
1 requires   2 needn't   3 must   4 permitted
5 needs   6 obliged   7 may not   8 should

Exercise 7
necessary: have to, must, need to, require, oblige
not necessary: don't have to, need not
against the rules: forbid, mustn't, not allowed
recommended or allowed: allow, supposed to,
permit, should

Exercise 8
1 c   2 e   3 f   4 b   5 g   6 d   7 h   8 a

Exercise 9
1 contractor   2 objective   3 bracket   4 scope
5 sample   6 deviation   7 durability   8 tailgate

Exercise 10
1 false   2 false   3 true   4 false   5 true   6 false
7 true   8 true

Exercise 13
1 hope   2 in regards to   3 unfortunately   4 due to
5 We would appreciate   6 do not hesitate
7 best regards

Exercise 14
Email 1
Greeting: Dear Mr. Martinez,
Small talk: I hope this email finds you well.
Reason for email: I am writing in regards to …
Request: We would appreciate …
Future contact: Do not hesitate to contact me if …
Sign off: Best regards,

Email 2
Greeting: Hello Markus,
Small talk: I hope you are doing well.
Reason for email: I'm writing about …
Request: Can you please …
Future contact: Feel free to get back to me if …
Sign off: Kind regards,

Exercise 15
1 e   2 f   3 d   4 c   5 a   6 b

Exercise 16
1 by   2 up   3 on   4 in   5 around
6 with (or no preposition)   7 out   8 off

Exercise 17
1 e   2 g   3 h   4 c   5 a   6 b   7 f   8 d

1   1e, 2g, 3h, 8d
2   4c, 5a, 6b, 7f

ANSWER KEY

UNIT 4

Exercise 1
1 scrap   2 knock on effect   3 bottleneck
4 shop floor   5 cycle time   6 stockpile
7 Machine operators   8 exceeds

Exercise 2
1 f defects   2 g overproduction   3 d waiting
4 b non-utilized talent   5 h motion
6 e inventory   7 c transportation
8 a extra processing

Exercise 4
1 discover   2 investigate   3 locate the cause of
4 come up with   5 consider different   6 decide on
7 implement   8 solve

Problems: to solve sth, to discover sth, to investigate
sth, to locate the cause of sth
Solutions: to come up with sth, to implement sth, to
consider different, to decide on sth

Exercise 5
Describing problems:
• Can we pinpoint what is causing this issue?
• How wide is the impact of the problem?
Finding solutions:
• Let's break down the problem.
• What if we tried a different approach? / How
  about considering an alternative solution?
Giving reasons:
• We lack the necessary resources to do this.
• While it's a great idea it doesn't align with our
  current strategy. / Great idea! It aligns with our
  current strategy.

Exercise 7
body shop   paint shop   press shop

1 blanks   2 assembly   3 welded   4 gaps
5 sealed   6 treatment   7 applied   8 cured

Exercise 9
1 e   2 d   3 f   4 b   5 a   6 c

Exercise 12
1 a   2 d   3 b   4 f   5 c   6 e

1 bonds, to   2 mounted on   3 clips, on
4 rivet, together   5 screws, to   6 bond, to

Exercise 13
1 torn   2 broken   3 scratch   4 loose   5 error
6 dent   7 doesn't work   8 fitting problem

UNIT 5

Warm-up
Company goals & program: introduce an employee
idea program
Compliance & regulations: meet emissions
standards
Production resources: reduce production waste
Products & materials: develop more environmentally
friendly vehicles

Exercise 1
1 fossil   2 greenhouse gases   3 recycle
4 renewable   5 greener   6 promote   7 reuse

Exercise 2
1 true   2 false   3 true   4 false   5 true   6 true
7 true   8 false

Exercise 3
1 meet   2 reaching   3 meet   4 meet
5 meet / reach   6 reach

Exercise 4
1 meet/reach, target
2 reach, agreement
3 reach, compromise
4 meet, regulations
5 meet, expectations
6 meet, milestone

Exercise 5
1 Objectives   2 pursue   3 challenge
4 fail to meet   5 achieve   6 track

Exercise 8
1 d speaking
Additional phrase: Li Wei, Nextron Motors.
2 c just calling
Additional phrase: I'm calling about …
3 h on track
Additional phrase: We are on schedule.
4 a the latest
Additional phrase: What is the current status?
5 f let's talk about
Additional phrase: Let's turn to …
6 g could be good to talk about
Additional phrase: How about another meeting soon?
7 b that covers
Additional phrase: Is there anything else to discuss?
8 e for calling
Additional phrase: I appreciate your call.

Exercise 11

1 g   2 a   3 d   4 b   5 f   6 h   7 c   8 e

Suggested answers:
1 There is more small talk and relationship building at the beginning of the phone call.
2 They better try to understand the priorities and needs of one another.
3 They try to come to a common understanding about the project goals in a collaborative way.

Exercise 12

Suggested answers:
1 Global EV sales since 2020 have had a dramatic increase.
2 In 2020 sales in Europe were higher than in China.
3 Compared with 2019, the sales in 2023 in the USA were substantially higher.
4 Sales figures in China in 2023 were about 8 million cars.

Exercise 13

1 compared to   2 achieved   3 profitability
4 reaching   5 market share   6 meeting   7 supply chains   8 sustainability   9 product portfolio

Exercise 14

1 e   2 f   3 a   4   5 c   6 d

UNIT 6 ──────────────────

Exercise 1

1 What factors are driving buying decisions?
2 New ways of connecting with customers
3 The power of video
4 Latest trends in digital marketing
5 Why digital marketing works

Exercise 2

1 brand loyalty   2 brand values   3 car subscription
4 customer engagement   5 immersive experience
6 media channels   7 touchpoints   8 SEO

Exercise 3

1 appeal   2 channels   3 convenience
4 touchpoints   5 showcase   6 showrooms
7 engagement   8 tailor

Suggested answers:
1 Advanced features like interior smart systems and autonomous driving
2 Television, print and media
3 Car subscriptions and shared mobility services
4 Search engine optimization (SEO) and digital marketing
5 Video platforms like YouTube
6 They allow buyers to explore different models, customize features and visualize their dream car in real-world settings.
7 New technologies like VR showrooms and AR-enabled apps
8 It allows carmakers to drive brand loyalty and car sales.

Exercise 4

Suggested answers:
1 SEO is very cost-effective
2 Share engaging content and build brand awareness
3 Showcase product features and communicate brand values
4 Promote brand to influencer followers

Exercise 5

1 f   2 d   3 a   4 e   5 b   6 c

Exercise 6

1 cutting-edge   2 engaged   3 10   4 500,000
5 merge   6 eco-friendly   7 6 million   8 300,000

Exercise 9

1 Value   2 **E**mpathize   3 inquiry   4 Acknowledge
5 Respond   6 Request

Exercise 10

to assist, to acknowledge, empathy, inquiry,
to request, to resolve, to respond, to value

Exercise 11

1 value   2 empathy   3 inquiry   4 acknowledge
5 resolve   6 respond to   7 assist   8 request

Exercise 12

Name: Rant
Model / Year: Z9 / 2024
Description of Problem: Steering wheel makes loud noises and gets stiff
Next Steps:
1 Plan a service appointment within 24 hours.
2 Arrange a courtesy car.

USEFUL PHRASES

The phrases below will be useful tools in your work. Highlight phrases which are particularly relevant to you and look at them regularly to help you remember them.

Additionally, you will find interactive exercises in the **Cornelsen Lernen App** expanding on the Useful Phrases provided in this book.

DESCRIBING YOUR WORK AND RESPONSIBILITIES

- I work in ... / the ... department.
- I'm responsible for ...
- One of my main tasks is ...
- I work closely with ...

- I deal with ...
- A lot has changed since ...
- I used to ... but now I ...

DESCRIBING PROCESSES

- Firstly ...
- Secondly ...
- Thirdly ...
- After that ...
- The next step is ...
- And then ...

- During this stage ...
- The main focus of the ... is ...
- The ... deals with ...
- Finally,
- The last stage is ...
- Last but not least is ...

LEADING DISCUSSIONS

Asking for opinions
- How do you feel about this?
- What's your opinion on ...?

Giving opinions
- In my mind ...
- As far as I'm concerned ...

Agreeing
- I agree with you on ...
- I feel the same way.

Disagreeing
- Sorry, I can't go along with you there.
- I'm afraid I see things differently.

Expressing agreement
- We are in agreement that ...
- We are all of the same opinion.

Redirecting a discussion
- I'm afraid we are getting off topic. Let's get back to ...
- The discussion is getting side-tracked.

Comparing ideas
- Let's look at the pros and cons of each idea.
- Let's compare the benefits and drawbacks.

Summarizing
- To sum up, ...
- In summary we can say that ...

HOLDING VIRTUAL MEETINGS

Welcoming participants
- Nice to meet you!
- Let's wait a few moments until everyone arrives.
- I think we can get started.

Connection issues
- Can everyone hear me okay?
- Sorry, I didn't catch that. The connection was bad.
- I am going to turn off my camera if that's OK.

Typical situations
- I'm afraid, your microphone is muted.
- Shall we use the hand signal when we want to speak?
- Could you post that in the chat, please?

Wrapping up
- Well, I think we've covered about everything, haven't we?
- Sorry, I have another meeting!
- Thanks everyone! Have a nice rest of the day!

OPENING AND CLOSING MEETINGS

Opening meetings
- Nice to see you all.
- Let's start with a round of introductions.
- Let's take a look at the agenda.
- Shall we move on to the first item?

Closing meetings
- If there is nothing else, I think we can wrap it up.
- Let's recap what we have agreed on …
- Thanks for all contributing, the meeting was really constructive.

MAKING SUGGESTIONS AND RECOMMENDATIONS

- How about trying a different solution?
- Why don't we move our work stations closer?
- By removing this step, we could save time.

- I'd recommend reducing your inventory.
- What about standardizing the process?
- If I were you, I'd clarify the responsibilities.
- Couldn't we simplify this process?

TALKING ABOUT PROBLEMS AND SOLUTIONS

Describing problems
- We need to find the cause of the problem.
- What about looking at the full impact / any knock-on effects?
- We should assess the problem in terms of money / time / energy / stress.
- Can we pinpoint what is causing this issue?
- How wide is the impact of the problem?

Finding solutions
- Shall we hear other solutions before making a decision?
- How about considering the problem from a different angle?
- Let's evaluate our ideas based on costs / effectiveness / time / energy.
- Let's break down the problem.
- What if we tried a different approach? / How about considering an alternative solution?

Giving reasons
- It seems this option is more cost-effective.
- This approach could be more time-saving / would be more time saving.
- It could be much easier to do it this way.
- I see your point, but this idea would be more time-consuming.
- I'm afraid this solution is much more cost-intensive.

- Doing it this way would be more labour-intensive.
- We lack the necessary resources to do this.
- While it's a great idea it doesn't align with our current strategy. / Great idea! It aligns with our current strategy.

USEFUL PHRASES

PRESENTING NUMBERS

Moving up & down
- Sales figures increased by …
- The number rose sharply / substantially by 5% …
- The amount dropped / fell in 2027 due to …
- Sales were higher / lower than …

Degree of change
- There was a dramatic / sharp increase in …
- In 2018 there was a substantial / significant decrease in …
- There was a small / minor drop in sales …

Remaining stable
- Sales were about / around / approximately …
- The number remained constant at …
- The total amount was just over / under …

COMPARING AND CONTRASTING INFORMATION

- Compared to/with video marketing, influencer marketing is …
- SMM is just as effective as …
- SEO is not as effective as …
- IM is more effective than …
- While VM impacts buyer decisions, it doesn't …

- Whereas SEO is cost-effective, it isn't …
- Although IM reaches a new audience, it isn't …
- SEO attracts potential buyers, however, it doesn't have the same impact as …

CONVINCING AND PERSUADING

Appealing to emotions
- Imagine if we …
- Think about the impact on …
- Look at the success we would have …

Giving reasons and examples
- We have to do this because …
- The most important factor is …
- There are many reasons why it's better. In particular …
- One example why it is …

Using data / facts
- It's a well-known fact that …
- The numbers show …
- Experts agree …

Personal experience
- In my experience …
- I've been in a similar situation before and would …
- Our last project showed that …

A

acceleration Beschleunigung
accelerator Gaspedal
accountability Verantwortung, Haftung
to **achieve sth** etw. erreichen
adhesion Haftverbund
advanced fortschrittlich
air vent Lüftungsdüsen
to **align sth with sth** etw. auf etw. ausrichten
all/four-wheel drive Allradantrieb
ambitious ehrgeizig
to **appeal to so** *hier:* jmdm. gefallen
appealing ansprechend
to **apply sth** etw. auftragen
A-pillar A-Säule
artificial künstlich
assembly Montage
autonomous autonom
awarding Vergabe

B

base model Basismodell
to **be adapted to sth** an etw. angepasst sein
to **be a gearhead** Benzin im Blut haben
to **be delighted** erfreut sein
to **be equipped with sth** mit etw. ausgestattet sein
to **be expected to do sth** es wird erwartet, dass ...
to **be fully-loaded** voll ausgebaut sein
to **be obliged to do sth** verpflichtet sein etw. zu tun
to **be on the right track** auf dem richtigen Weg sein
blank Zuschnitt
blind spot toter Winkel
bottleneck Engpass
boundary conditions Randbedingungen
brake pedal Bremspedal
brand value Markenwert

C

cabin Fahrgastraum
to **capture sth** etw. erfassen
carbon footprint ökologischer Fußabdruck
carbon-neutral CO2-neutral

car subscription Fahrzeugabonnement
center console Mittelkonsole
charging time Ladezeit
commission Provision, Gebühr
commitment *hier:* Engagement
competition Wettbewerb
to **competitive** wettbewerbsfähig
comprehensive umfassend
constraint Einschränkung
to **consult** beraten
contingency plan Notfallplan
to **convey sth** *hier:* etw. transportieren
crucial wichtig
to **cure sth** *hier:* etw. aushärten
customer engagement Kund*innenbindung
customization Anpassung, Personalisierung
cycle time Taktzeit

D

data ownership Datenbesitz
dashboard Armaturenbrett
day-to-day work tägliche Arbeit
to **delegate sth** etw. delegieren
deliverables (pl.) Projektergebnisse
derivative Derivat, Modellvariante
die *hier:* Pressform
directions (pl.) Wegbeschreibung
disruption Störung, Unterbrechung
door trim Türverkleidung
drag coefficient Luftwiderstandsbeiwert
driver seat Fahrersitz

E

economies of scale (pl) Skaleneffekte
electric elektrisch
electric vehicle (EV) Elektrofahrzeug
emerging markets Schwellenmarkt
to **emit sth** etw. ausstoßen
environmentally conscious umweltbewusst
equipment *hier:* Betriebsmittel
to **estimate** einschätzen

to **exceed sth** etw. überschreiten
to **expand sth** etw. ausweiten
to **exploit so/sth** jmdn./etw. ausbeuten

F

facility Einrichtung
to **facilitate sth** etw. moderieren
feasibility Machbarkeit
fender Kotflügel
fleet customer Großkunde
to **fluctuate** schwanken
fossil fuels fossile Brennstoffe
to **foster sth** etw. fördern
footwell Fußraum
freeze Sperre, "Freeze"
front-wheel drive Vorderradantrieb
to **fulfill sth** etw. erfüllen

G

gamechanger bahnbrechende Änderung
gap *hier:* Fuge, Spaltmaß
gasoline (AE) / **petrol** (BE) Benzin
getaway Ausflug
global warming globale Erwärmung
glove compartment Handschuhfach
greener umweltfreundlicher
greenhouse gases Treibhausgase
grille Kühlergrill, Gitter

H

harmful schädlich
headliner Himmel
headroom Kopffreiheit
hidden expenses versteckte Kosten
high-end model Spitzenmodell
high-resolution hochauflösend
horn Hupe
hurdle Hürde

I

instrument cluster Instrumententafel
interest rate Zinssatz
in terms of sth hinsichtlich etw.

L

lane departure assistant Spurhaltesystem
leeway Spielraum
lift coefficient Auftriebsbeiwert
lineup Produktreihe
loan Darlehen

M

markup Aufpreis
meeting minutes (pl.) Protokoll
merger Fusion
merit *hier:* Leistung
to **mitigate sth** etw. abmildern

N

need Bedürfnis

O

objective kurzfristiges Ziel
on the fly spontan, ohne Vorbereitung
operational betrieblich
to **optimize sth** etw. optimieren
original equipment manufacturer (OEM) Automobilhersteller
to **overburden sth** etw. überlasten
to **overtake sth** etw. überholen

P

packaging *hier:* Platznutzungskonzept
to **participate in sth** an etw. teilnehmen
part sample Musterteil
passenger seat Beifahrersitz
pearl chain Perlenkette
to **postpone sth until** etw. verschieben auf
pothole Schlagloch
powertrain Antrieb
predecessor Vorgängermodell
primer Grundierung
procurement department Einkauf
purchasing Einkauf
purchasing release Einkaufsfreigabe
to **pursue sth** etw. verfolgen, anstreben

R

range anxiety Reichweitenangst
range extension Reichweitenverlängerung
rear bumper hinterer Stoßfänger
rear-view mirror Rückspiegel
rear-wheel drive Hinterradantrieb
recommendation Empfehlung
renewable erneuerbar
request Anfrage
requirement Anforderung
to **reschedule sth** etw. umplanen, verlegen
reskilling Umschulen
reusable wiederverwendbar
to **rework sth** etw. überarbeiten

S

scheduling conflict Terminkollision
scope Umfang
to **scrap sth** etw. verschrotten
seam Naht
seamless nahtlos
search engine optimization (SEO) Suchmaschinenoptimierung
to **secure sth** etw. sichern
self-driving selbstfahrend
shop floor Produktionsstätte
shortage Knappheit
sloping abfallend
to **showcase sth** etw. zur Schau stellen
showroom Ausstellungsraum
sophisticated ausgefeilt
specification manual Lastenheft
staffing Besetzung
to **stamp sth** *hier:* etw. stanzen
to **stay ahead of the curve** der Zeit voraus sein
to **stockpile sth** etw. bevorraten
struggle Ringen, Kampf
styling Design
to **submit sth** etw. unterbreiten, vorlegen
successor Nachfolgermodell
to **suit so** jmdm. zeitlich passen
suitable passend, geeignet
sun visor Sonnenblende
supply chain Lieferkette
to **swap sth** etw. austauschen

T

to **tailor sth** etw. maßschneidern
tailpipe Auspuffrohr
to **take a day off** einen Tag freinehmen
to **tighten sth** etw. verschärfen
touchpoint Berührungspunkt
to **track sth** etw. verfolgen
treatment Behandlung
trolley Wagen

U

ultimately letztendlich
unevenness Ungleichmäßigkeit
unforeseen unvorhersehbar
to **utilize sth** etw. verwerten, verwenden

V

to **validate sth** etw. bestätigen, genehmigen
value chain Wertschöpfungskette

W

wear and tear Verschleiß
to **weld sth** etw. schweißen
whereas wohingegen
widespread weit verbreitet
wind tunnel Windkanal
windscreen angle Winkel der Windschutzscheibe

GLOSSARY

German	American English	British English
	Vehicles	
Geländewagen, SUV	SUV	4X4
Kabriolett	convertible	convertible, cabriolet
Kombi	station wagon	estate
Lastwagen	truck	lorry
Limousine	sedan	saloon
Minivan	minivan	MPV
Wohnmobil	mobile home, recreational vehicle	camper van
Wohnwagen	trailer	caravan
	Car parts	
Antenne	antenna	aerial
Batterie	battery	accumulator
Blinker	turn signal	indicator
Getriebe	transmission	gearbox
Kofferraum	trunk	boot
Kotflügel	fender	wing
Motorhaube	hood	bonnet
Nummernschild	license plate	number plate
Profil	tread	track
Radkappe	hubcap	nave plate
Reifen	tire	tyre
Schalldämpfer	muffler	silencer
Schalthebel	gear shift	gear stick
Scheibenwischer	windshield wiper	windscreen wiper
Schweller	rocker panel	sill
Windschutzscheibe	windshield	windscreen
	Automotive vocabulary	
Autobahn	highway, freeway	motorway
Autovermietung	car rental	car hire
Benzin	gas	petrol
Bürgersteig, Gehweg	sidewalk	pavement
Führerschein	driver's license	driving licence
Kreisverkehr	traffic circle	roundabout
Kreuzung	intersection	crossroads
Parkplatz	parking lot	car park
Zebrastreifen	crosswalk	pedestrian crossing